Cambridge English

EMPOWER

INTERMEDIATE
WORKBOOK
WITH ANSWERS

B1+

Peter Anderson

Contents

1A Keeping in touch

1 GRAMMAR
Subject and object questions

a <u>Underline</u> the correct words to complete the questions.

1 Who *did he write* / <u>*wrote*</u> the play *Romeo and Juliet*?
2 Which tooth *does it hurt* / *hurts* when I touch it?
3 What *did it happen* / *happened* after the police arrived?
4 Which football match *did they watch* / *watched* on TV last night?
5 Which book *did you talk* / *talked* about in your English class?
6 Who *did he talk* / *talked* to at the party last night?
7 Which student *did she get* / *got* the highest marks in the test?
8 Who *did you vote* / *voted* for at the last election?

b Put the words in the correct order to make questions.

1 you / who / that / gave / book / your birthday / for ?
<u>Who gave you that book for your birthday?</u>
2 parents / to / your / which / did / restaurant / go ?
_____
3 Harrison Ford / of / happens / the end / at / the film / what / to ?
_____
4 did / you and / about / friends / your / talk / what ?
_____
5 like / your / first / mobile phone / was / what ?
_____
6 his / about / was / what / presentation ?
_____
7 married / twice / film / got / year / star / last / which ?
_____
8 who / you / to / did / cinema / the / with / go ?
_____

2 VOCABULARY Communication

a Complete the sentences with the words in the box.

presentation   interviewed   expressing   in public
opinions   joke   ~~face-to-face~~   in touch

1 I prefer having *face-to-face* meetings with my colleagues, rather than talking to them on the phone.
2 She used her laptop to give an extremely clear _____ of her project in class.
3 Our teacher always tells a _____ at the beginning of each lesson. Sometimes they're quite funny; sometimes they're terrible.
4 Although I left the country fifteen years ago, I still keep _____ with some of my old friends.
5 The politician was _____ by a journalist from *The Times*.
6 He isn't very good at _____ his feelings. He's rather shy so I never know if he's happy or not.
7 She doesn't usually say much in meetings. I don't think she likes speaking _____.
8 David's a very direct person. He always gives his _____ about my paintings.

b <u>Underline</u> the correct words to complete the sentences.

1 I *complained* / *argued* / *persuaded* to the waiter that my food wasn't hot enough.
2 I said I would take a taxi to the airport but they *complained* / *insisted* / *kept* on driving me in their car.
3 We were *argued* / *encouraged* / *greeted* at the airport by the Minister of Tourism.
4 He *argued* / *expressed* / *persuaded* her to lend him the £500 he needed to buy a new TV.
5 My father *argued* / *encouraged* / *expressed* me to apply for the job although I had very little experience in that area.
6 My husband and I always *argue* / *complain* / *insist* about where to go on holiday. I prefer the beach while he prefers the mountains.
7 The babysitter *argued* / *complained* / *persuaded* the children to go to bed at 9 o'clock.
8 Our teacher *complained* / *encouraged* / *persuaded* us to read English and American newspapers online.

B I'm using an app for learning English

1 GRAMMAR
Present simple and continuous

a Match 1–8 with a–h to make sentences and questions.

1 [g] They play
2 [ ] He's thinking
3 [ ] She's going
4 [ ] I'm having
5 [ ] He thinks
6 [ ] We go
7 [ ] I have
8 [ ] They're playing

a a yoga class on Monday evenings.
b to school on Saturday mornings in my country.
c tennis in the park. Why don't you go and join them?
d about all the things he needs to do before his holiday.
e my dinner now so can I call you back in ten minutes?
f that his children will live until they are 100 years old.
g chess with their grandad every Sunday after lunch.
h to work by bike at the moment because she wants to get fit.

b Complete the conversation with the present simple or present continuous form of the verbs in brackets. Use contractions where possible.

ARTHUR ¹Is Emma doing (Emma, do) well at school these days?
PAT Yes, she is.
ARTHUR ² _____ (she, study) languages, like her brother?
PAT Yes, she ³ _____ (learn) French and Spanish.
ARTHUR Really? ⁴ _____ (she, want) to become an interpreter?
PAT She ⁵ _____ (not, know) yet. She ⁶ _____ (be) only 14, after all.
ARTHUR Yes, that's true. And what about sport? ⁷ _____ (she, play) a lot of sport at school?
PAT Yes, she ⁸ _____ (love) all sports. She ⁹ _____ (be) particularly good at basketball. In fact, she ¹⁰ _____ (play) for the school team in a match today.
ARTHUR Really? Great!
PAT Hold on … er, my phone ¹¹ _____ (ring) …
ARTHUR Who is it?
PAT It's my husband. Sorry, I must go – he ¹² _____ (wait) for me in the car.
ARTHUR OK, bye!

2 VOCABULARY
Gradable and extreme adjectives

a Match 1–8 with a–h to make sentences.

1 [f] I hate swimming in the North Sea because
2 [ ] I thought the book was brilliant, probably the best detective story
3 [ ] After we'd walked 25 km
4 [ ] They gave him such an enormous portion of spaghetti that
5 [ ] Lots of tourists had just left their rubbish behind them so
6 [ ] I asked her to open the window because
7 [ ] If you're late for his class again
8 [ ] We all thought the play was awful so

a I felt absolutely exhausted.
b the beach was absolutely filthy.
c even he couldn't finish it.
d it was boiling in there.
e I've ever read.
f the water's always freezing.
g we left the theatre at the interval.
h he'll be furious!

b Complete the sentences with the words in the box.

tiny   impossible   fantastic   delicious
miserable   freezing   useless   filthy

1 We had a ___fantastic___ holiday in Bali. The weather was lovely, the hotel was perfect and the beaches were beautiful.
2 The weather was _____ when I was in Moscow last week – minus 15° during the day!
3 He's renting a _____ flat in the centre of Paris – it's only got one room!
4 The children looked so _____ when their pet rabbit died.
5 He spoke so quickly it was _____ to understand what he was saying.
6 Nobody had cleaned the kitchen for months. It was absolutely _____.
7 Thanks for a lovely dinner. The seafood risotto was absolutely _____. You must give me the recipe.
8 My football team are completely _____. We lost our last match 6 – 0.

1 USEFUL LANGUAGE
Giving and responding to opinions

a Complete the exchanges with the words in the box.

guess	sure	see	concerned	mean	opinion	ask	think

1 **A** Well, if you ___*ask*___ me, Tanya Davies would be the best person for the job.
   B Actually, I don't agree. As far as I'm _____, Luke Adams would be better.
2 **A** Well, I _____ you could take the shoes back to the shop.
   B I'm not so _____ about that. I've already worn them.
3 **A** I _____ it's going to be difficult to make enough money to survive.
   B Yes, I _____ where you're coming from. Maybe we should find a cheaper office?
4 **A** Well, in my _____, Italian is easier than French.
   B I know what you _____. I think it's easier to pronounce.

b ▶ **1.1** Listen and check.

c Underline the correct words to complete the sentences.

1 **A** It *comes* / *means* / *seems* to me that their coffee is better than ours.
   B Yes, I know exactly what you *mean* / *opinion* / *think*. It's really smooth, isn't it?
2 **A** As far as *I'm concerned* / *I guess* / *my opinion*, I think it makes sense to take the train to Paris.
   B I'm not so *mean* / *right* / *sure* about that. It takes nearly three hours.
3 **A** I *mean* / *sure* / *think* Germany will probably win the football World Cup.
   B Yes, I think that's *mean* / *right* / *sure*. They've got the best team.
4 **A** Well, in my *ask* / *guess* / *opinion*, we need to find another business partner in Spain.
   B Yes, I see *what* / *where* / *why* you're coming from. Maybe a company based in Madrid this time?

d ▶ **1.2** Listen and check.

2 PRONUNCIATION
Word groups

a ▶ **1.3** Listen to the exchanges and underline the word you hear before each speaker pause

1 **A** Guess what, Tony? I've just read about this girl, and she's only ten but she's fluent in several different languages.
   B That's fantastic. I can only speak one language – English.
2 **A** Hi, Linda. Are you learning Russian?
   B I'm trying to! But this book's useless! It teaches you how to say 'my uncle's black trousers' but not how to say 'hello'!

D Skills for Writing
Different ways of learning

1 READING

a Read the text and tick (✓) the best ending for the sentence.

If you want to be a good photographer, …

a ☐ you shouldn't take lots of photos.
b ☐ you shouldn't use your smartphone.
c ☐ you don't need to study the manual.
d ☐ you should always take your camera with you when you go out.

b Read the text again. Are the sentences true or false?

1 With a digital camera or smartphone it is easier to take good photos than 20 years ago.
2 You shouldn't use automatic mode when you start using a new camera.
3 It is better not to take many photos when you are learning how to use a camera.
4 Your family and friends will be more relaxed if you take lots of photos.
5 It is easy to take good photos of people using the flash on your camera.

2 WRITING SKILLS Introducing a purpose; Referring pronouns

a <u>Underline</u> the correct words to complete the sentences.

1 *For improving* / *Improving* / <u>*To improve*</u> your listening skills, it's a good idea to watch films in English.
2 You should write a sentence that includes the new word *in order* / *to* / *so that* you can remember it more easily.
3 It's better to use a monolingual dictionary. *These* / *This* / *Those* will help you to start thinking in English.
4 Some people prefer to write the new words on cards with the translation. *That* / *These* / *This* technique will help you to remember what the word means and how it is spelt.
5 There are lots of things you can do *in order* / *so* / *that* to become a better language learner.
6 Why don't you practise repeating the questions that you hear on the DVD-ROM *so* / *that* / *to* you learn the correct intonation?

3 WRITING

a Read the notes. Write a guide on how to be a better cook.

Notes for 'How to improve your cookery skills'

1) Introduction: How to become a good cook
  • Try new dishes. Practise.
  • Don't repeat same dishes all the time.
2) Learn new dishes
  • Buy recipe books.
  • Test on family/close friends first. Larger groups later.
  • Try new recipes 2–3 times a week.
  • Ask family/friends for honest opinions. Make improvements.
3) Watch TV cookery programmes
  • Easy way to follow recipe. Watch & download recipes from website.
4) Share recipes
  • Enjoyed a good meal? Ask for recipe. Will discover new dishes & improve.

Read article Edit Comment

How to take better photos

👁 1,843,076 views ✏ Edited **5 days ago**

These days it is much easier to become a good photographer because of the big improvements in camera technology over the past 20 years. In order to take good photos you need to have a good digital camera or a smartphone with a good camera.

Make sure you read the manual carefully before you start using your camera. This will help you to understand the most important functions, such as how to use the flash and the zoom. Putting the camera in automatic mode is a good way to make sure you don't make too many mistakes while you are still unfamiliar with how your camera works.

It is a good idea to take your camera with you at all times so that you are always ready to take a photo whenever you see something interesting. Try to take as many photos as possible. This will help you to get better at using your camera and will result in better photos. Remember the saying 'Practice makes perfect'. The more you practise taking photos, the better you will become.

If you take lots of photos of your family and friends, in the end they will forget about the camera and feel more relaxed when you take photos of them. This will help you to take photos that look more natural and less posed.

To get the best photos of people you need to be outdoors, as the light outside is much better. It is extremely difficult to take attractive photos of people indoors using flash, so it is always better to be outside when you photograph people.

7

UNIT 1
Reading and listening extension

1 READING

a Read part of an introduction to a textbook for students. Are the sentences true or false?

The writer of this textbook believes that …

1 teachers in many countries expect their students to speak perfect English.
2 her book is for students who want to improve their English in a short time.
3 phrases that seem to be similar can sometimes communicate opposite meanings.
4 students may sound rude in English if they do not learn to speak the language perfectly.
5 we can understand someone more easily when we think about the culture that they come from.

b Read the text again. Match the words in bold in 1–7 with the things they refer to in a–g.

1 [e] By **this**, they mean that …
2 [ ] … **that** might seem strange
3 [ ] … someone gives **them** a present.
4 [ ] *Why did you get me **this**?*
5 [ ] Why is **this**?
6 [ ] And in fact, **this** phrase (or something like **it**) …
7 [ ] … different cultures say **them** in different ways …

a A birthday present.
b Ideas which are similar to each other.
c People from English-speaking countries.
d Saying *Oh, you didn't need to get me anything!*
e Speaking English perfectly.
f *Why did you get me this?*
g Why one phrase is rude but the other one is polite.

c Write a short email to the students in your class about learning English. Your email should:

• introduce yourself (your name, where you come from)
• explain why you are learning English
• describe where you have learned English in the past
• say what you hope to learn on this course.

Use the phrases below to help you.

Hi! My name's … and I'm from …
I'm learning English because I *want to … / need to … / am going to …*
I have been learning English *for* + [AMOUNT OF TIME] / *since* + [POINT IN TIME]
I started learning English *at school / when I was* + [AGE]
On this course, I really want to improve my …

A Beginner's Guide to
INTERCULTURAL COMMUNICATION

A personal goal for many students is to be able to speak English perfectly. By **this**, they mean that they would like to be able to tell a joke or feel completely confident in a face-to-face conversation with a group of native speakers. Any student can achieve this goal (and many do) but it takes many, *many* years of study.

If just the thought of all those years of study makes you feel exhausted, then the book you are now holding in your hands may be for you. *A Beginner's Guide to Intercultural Communication* has been written to help students who are learning English answer the question 'What are the best ways to communicate in a foreign language?'

But first of all let's think about what communication actually means. In our first language, we know that we have to choose our words very carefully. For example, I'm from Australia so when someone gives me a birthday present, I might say:

Oh, you didn't need to get me anything!

If you are not a native English speaker, **that** might seem strange. But many English speakers feel it is polite to say this when someone gives **them** a present. However, the same speakers would find it quite rude to say:

*Why did you get me **this**?*

Why is **this**? After all, the meaning of both phrases is quite similar. And in fact, **this** phrase (or something like **it**) is quite common in a number of European languages. The answer is simple – whether something seems to be rude or polite depends on culture. To communicate successfully in a foreign language, we need to remember that people are usually trying to say the same things but we also need to remember that different cultures say **them** in different ways – and that is what intercultural communication is all about.

2 LISTENING

a ▶ 1.4 Listen to a conversation between Bridget and Joe and tick (✓) the correct answers.

1 What is the main topic of their conversation?
   a ☐ the subject Bridget studies at university
   b ☐ a holiday that Bridget has had
   c ☐ a website that Bridget is creating

2 Bridget is feeling very tired because she has …
   a ☐ been writing something in a foreign language.
   b ☐ had a lot of essays to write for university.
   c ☐ just returned from a holiday in Mexico.

3 Bridget wants Joe to help her to …
   a ☐ check her grammar and spelling.
   b ☐ design a website.
   c ☐ improve her Spanish.

4 Bridget shows Joe a photo of a place in …
   a ☐ Egypt.
   b ☐ Mexico.
   c ☐ Singapore.

b Listen again. Underline the correct words to complete the sentences.

1 Bridget has *just started* / *almost finished* / *stopped working on* her website.

2 At her university, Bridget is a student in the *French and Spanish* / *Latin American studies* / *Culture and Politics* department.

3 Bridget's website is for students at her own university and also for students *all around the world* / *in Colombia* / *in Mexico*.

4 *A professor* / *Another student* / *Nobody else* has helped Bridget to write the information she needs for her website.

5 Chichen Itza is the name of *a building* / *a city* / *a university* they can see in her photo.

6 Joe thinks the photo of Chichen Itza is *absolutely perfect* / *the wrong size* / *too old-fashioned* for Bridget's website.

c Write a conversation between two people planning a website for your English class. Think about these questions:
   • what information students need (e.g. homework, vocabulary)
   • how the information will be organised
   • who will create the website.

⊙ Review and extension

1 GRAMMAR

Correct the sentences.

1 What time started the football match?
   What time did the football match start?
2 My brother isn't liking coffee.
3 How was your holiday in Spain like?
4 Look at Tom – he wears his new shoes.
5 Who did take you to the station?
6 Can you repeat that? I'm not understanding.

2 VOCABULARY

Correct the sentences.

1 You've just walked 20 kilometres – you must be exausted.
   You've just walked 20 kilometres – you must be exhausted.
2 When we were young my brother and I used to discuss all the time, but now we've become good friends.
3 It's imposible to sleep because my neighbours are having a party.
4 I haven't rested in touch with many of my old school friends.
5 That cake was delicius but there was only a tiny piece left!
6 My dad is very funny. He loves making jokes about his time in the army.

3 WORDPOWER *yourself*

Complete the sentences with the verbs in the box.

enjoy   help   ~~hurt~~   do   teach   look after

1 Hello, Grandma. I'm sorry you fell over while you were shopping. It's lucky you didn't ____*hurt*____ yourself.
2 _____ yourself to a hot drink. There's some fresh coffee and tea in the kitchen.
3 Have a great time at the party! _____ yourself.
4 You don't need to go to classes to learn a foreign language. You can _____ yourself using books and a DVD.
5 Make sure you _____ yourself while I'm away. Eat plenty of food and get enough sleep.
6 You don't need to pay someone to paint your bedroom. It isn't hard. You can _____ it yourself.

⟳ REVIEW YOUR PROGRESS

Look again at Review your progress on p.18 of the Student's Book. How well can you do these things now?
3 = very well   2 = well   1 = not so well

I CAN …

talk about different forms of communication	☐
describe experiences in the present	☐
give and respond to opinions	☐
write a guide.	☐

2A They've just offered me the job

1 GRAMMAR Present perfect simple and past simple

a Underline the correct words to complete the exchanges.

1 **A** How long *were you* / *have you been* at your present company?

   B *I worked* / *I've worked* for them since 2012.

2 **A** *Did you ever arrive* / *Have you ever arrived* late for a job interview?

   B Yes, last month, because of a delay on the train. *I arrived* / *I've arrived* there two hours late!

3 **A** *Did she ever work* / *Has she ever worked* in another country?

   B Yes, *she spent* / *she's spent* nine months in our Madrid office in 2008.

4 **A** *Matt applied* / *Matt's applied* for 20 jobs since January.

   B Yes and he *didn't have* / *hasn't had* any interviews yet.

5 **A** *Did you meet* / *Have you met* your new boss yet?

   B Yes, *I met* / *I've met* her for the first time yesterday.

b Complete the conversation with the present perfect or past simple form of the verbs in brackets. Use contractions where possible.

A [1]<u>Have you worked</u> (you, work) for a television company before?

B Yes, [2]I _____ (work) for three different companies since I finished university. Immediately after university I [3]_____ (get) a job with MTV.

A OK, so can you tell us something about your job at MTV?

B Yes, of course. What would you like to know?

A How long [4]_____ (you, stay) at MTV?

B I [5]_____ (stay) there for five years, from 2006 to 2011.

A Five years? And what [6]_____ (you, like) most about the job?

B I really [7]_____ (enjoy) being in charge of a team. It [8]_____ (give) me some useful experience of managing other people.

A And now you're working at the BBC. So how long [9]_____ (you, be) with the BBC?

B I [10]_____ (be) in my current job for two years.

A So how much experience [11]_____ (you, have) of children's TV since you [12]_____ (join) the BBC?

B I [13]_____ (be) the editor of *The Magic Garden* for the last nine months.

2 VOCABULARY Work

a Match 1–8 with a–h to make sentences.

1 [e] Steve and Kevin both applied for
2 [ ] We've invited four of the candidates for
3 [ ] At conferences, I try to meet lots of people. It's good to have
4 [ ] She's a manager now and she's in charge of
5 [ ] Honda are one of the biggest employers in the region, with
6 [ ] He's studying photography at university and he'd like to have
7 [ ] I've been a teacher for 20 years so I've got a lot of
8 [ ] I've got good problem-solving

a a career in television or films.
b business contacts from other organisations.
c a second interview next Monday and Tuesday.
d experience in education.
e the job but only Kevin was invited for an interview.
f a team of five sales representatives.
g skills, so I can usually find a solution when things go wrong.
h over 2,000 employees in their new car factory.

b Complete the sentences with the words in the box.

grades   apply   charge   experience
~~career~~   team   interview   CV

1 My uncle had a long ___career___ in the army.
2 Philip has just been promoted. He's now in _____ of the marketing department at work.
3 I work in a _____ of five people.
4 They've invited me for an _____ next week.
5 When you write a _____, it's best to put all the information on a maximum of two pages.
6 I have fifteen years' _____ in hotel management.
7 My brother got excellent _____ at school.
8 Why don't you _____ for a job as a journalist?

3 PRONUNCIATION Present perfect simple and past simple

a ▶2.1 Listen to the sentences. Which sentence do you hear? Tick (✓) the correct box.

1 a [✓] I applied for lots of jobs.
   b [ ] I've applied for lots of jobs.

2 a [ ] We worked very hard today.
   b [ ] We've worked very hard today.

3 a [ ] I learned a lot in this job.
   b [ ] I've learnt a lot in this job.

4 a [ ] They offered me more money.
   b [ ] They've offered me more money.

5 a [ ] You had a fantastic career at the BBC.
   b [ ] You've had a fantastic career at the BBC.

I've been playing on my phone all morning

1 GRAMMAR Present perfect simple and continuous

a Complete the sentences with the present perfect continuous form of the verbs in the box. Use contractions where possible.

| cry | learn | go | post | wait | read | cook | ~~play~~ |

1 I feel exhausted because I *'ve been playing* tennis all afternoon.
2 We _____ at the station for half an hour but my dad's train hasn't arrived yet.
3 She _____ a lot of messages on Facebook lately.
4 My eyes feel really tired. I _____ all day.
5 Dad _____ for hours. He's made an enormous meal.
6 You look really upset. _____ you _____?
7 My kids _____ Spanish for four years and now they can understand nearly everything.
8 How long _____ Neil _____ out with his girlfriend?

b <u>Underline</u> the correct verb forms to complete the sentences and questions.

1 *Dan's been using* / *Dan's used* his phone a lot recently to take photos of his children.
2 *I've been installing* / *I've installed* the new program and it's working perfectly.
3 Have you *been turning off* / *turned off* your phone? The film's starting now.
4 My computer *hasn't been working* / *hasn't worked* properly recently. I think something's wrong.
5 *You've been playing* / *You've played* that computer game all afternoon. Can you stop for five minutes, please?
6 How long have you *been waiting* / *waited* for your computer to install that weather app?
7 *I've been having* / *I've had* this tablet for three years and it still works perfectly.
8 *We've been trying* / *We've tried* to call Fiona on her mobile phone all day but she's not answering.

2 VOCABULARY Technology

a <u>Underline</u> the correct words to complete the sentences.

1 You can *download* / *upload* ebooks onto your tablet and then read them while you're on holiday.
2 Your *password* / *browser* should be a combination of letters, numbers and other characters.
3 Please help us to save energy by turning *on* / *off* your computer when you leave the office.
4 I've just found an amazing new *icon* / *app* which translates pop songs from English to Portuguese.
5 You can *share* / *delete* your photos with your family and friends on our new photo management website.
6 I think I *pressed* / *deleted* your email by mistake so could you send it to me again?
7 If you *click* / *type* on this button, it opens the program.
8 Why don't you *upload* / *download* a more recent profile photo on your homepage?
9 You're *clicking* / *typing* the wrong letters because the CAPS LOCK button is on.
10 When you enter the system, you need to enter your unique *username* / *icon*, which in your case is johnsmith.

b Complete the crossword puzzle.

```
                    [1]              [2]
         [3]C  L  I [4]C  K       [5]

              [6]

     [7]                          [8]
```

→ Across

3 To visit our website, please ___*click*___ on this link.
6 If you _____ this app, we'll be able to use our phones to have video calls.
7 To surf the Internet, you need to have a _____ such as Internet Explorer or Google Chrome.
8 To log onto your account, you have to _____ your username and password.

↓ Down

1 We'd love to see your photos from the party. Can you _____ them onto Facebook so we can all see them?
2 It's quicker to send a text _____ to your friends than to send them an email.
4 If you are in a café with wi-fi, you can _____ your laptop or tablet to the Internet.
5 If you don't recognise the sender of an email, you should _____ it as it might be dangerous.

1 USEFUL LANGUAGE
Making suggestions

a <u>Underline</u> the correct words to complete the sentences.

1 Could you *ask* / *asking* your brother to help you?
2 Oh, really? That's a *dear* / *shame*.
3 How about *take* / *taking* it back to the shop where you bought it?
4 I'm really *brilliant* / *glad* to hear that.
5 Why don't you try *talk* / *talking* to your boss about it?
6 Let's *take* / *taking* it to the garage.
7 Oh dear. How *annoy* / *annoying*!
8 Shall we *ask* / *asking* his girlfriend what kind of music he likes?

b ▶2.2 Listen and check.

c Complete the words.

GARY I'm moving to a new flat next week but I don't know how to move all my things. Look at all these boxes!
KAREN How about ¹j<u>ust</u> hiring a car?
GARY No, that's too expensive.
KAREN ²W_____ about ordering a taxi?
GARY That's ³w_____ a try but there are a lot of things here. We might need three trips in a taxi. That's not going to be cheap.
KAREN No, it isn't. Have you ⁴t_____ asking a friend to drive you?
GARY I'll ⁵g_____ it a try but all my friends are students. Nobody has a car.
KAREN Oh, I know! Susie's mum has a flower shop and they have a van. You could get all your things in it and she could drive you to the new flat. ⁶S_____ I ask her to help?
GARY That's a great ⁷i_____!
KAREN Cool! Hey, ⁸I_____ invite her for dinner tonight and we can ask her then.
GARY Sure. Why ⁹n_____?
KAREN Great. ¹⁰C_____ you go to the supermarket and get some food, and I'll call her now?
GARY OK. Thanks, Karen.
KAREN No problem, Gary. You know what they say. Two heads are better than one!

d Put the conversation in the correct order.

☐ **B** Oh, no. How awful!
☐ **B** That's brilliant! I'm so pleased!
☐ **A** OK … No, it isn't in there …
☐ **A** Oh, listen – it's ringing! It's behind that cushion on the sofa!
☐ **A** I've been looking for it everywhere. I'm sure I had it when I got home.
☐ **A** That's a great idea. I'll give it a try. Can I borrow your phone for a minute?
☐ **B** OK, so it isn't in your bag. Have you tried phoning your number from another phone?
[1] **A** I've lost my phone!
☐ **B** What about checking in your bag?
☐ **B** Yes, sure. Here you are.

e ▶2.3 Listen and check.

2 PRONUNCIATION Sentence stress

a ▶2.4 Listen to the sentences and <u>underline</u> the stressed syllables.

1 <u>Barbara's</u> just <u>bought</u> a new <u>car</u> and it <u>won't start</u>!
2 My boss has been criticising my work recently.
3 My neighbours had a party last night so I didn't sleep very well.
4 My computer's been running very slowly since I installed that new program.

1 READING

a Read the text and tick (✓) the correct answer.

a ☐ Francesca has found a job with an advertising agency in London.
b ☐ Francesca is going to join a rock band in London.
c ☐ Francesca is going to begin her new job in London in April.
d ☐ Francesca is going to work in a hotel in the centre of London.

Inbox 📁 🗑 ✉

Hi Anna

I'm sorry I didn't reply to your last email straightaway but I've been very busy for the last two weeks.

I've been travelling from Manchester to London most days for job interviews. I've had interviews with some major advertising agencies and marketing companies and it's been great to make so many business contacts in London.

You'll never believe this, but Outreach Marketing have just emailed me to offer me a job in their offices in Covent Garden. The job sounds brilliant! They want me to be in charge of a team that helps to promote some well-known pop stars and rock bands. And what's really amazing is that they also want me to find new singers and bands that we could promote in the future.

They've made me a fantastic job offer. Apart from giving me a really good salary they're also going to give me a company car. But the best thing is that they've agreed to pay for me to stay in a hotel in Central London for a month while I look for a flat to rent. Besides going to lots of free concerts, I'll also be able to visit all the museums and art galleries I've read about. I've accepted the offer and am going to start my new job at the beginning of April. I can't wait!

Everyone says that London's a fantastic city so I'm really looking forward to living there. We must get together before I leave, so why don't we meet up for coffee in the next two or three weeks? Let me know a day that suits you.

Best wishes

Francesca

b Read the text again. Are the sentences true or false?

1 Francesca has been to London several times in the last two weeks.
2 Francesca didn't meet any important people in London.
3 Francesca is going to be a manager in a marketing company.
4 Outreach Marketing aren't interested in promoting new singers or bands.
5 Francesca has already found a flat to rent in London.
6 Francesca thinks that it will be nice to live in London.

2 WRITING SKILLS
Adding new information

a Match 1–6 with a–f to make sentences.

1 ☐f Besides its wonderful beaches,
2 ☐ In addition to my teaching experience in the UK,
3 ☐ I've worked as a pilot for an American airline
4 ☐ Besides agreeing to pay for four flights back to the UK each year
5 ☐ I have excellent technical qualifications.
6 ☐ Apart from paying me a higher salary they're

a apart from Flexi Airlines.
b In addition, I speak three languages fluently.
c they've also agreed to pay for my family to fly to Dubai once a year.
d also going to give me a company car.
e I've also worked in a primary school in South Africa for two years.
f Sicily also has lots of interesting historical sites.

3 WRITING

a Read the notes. Write an email to Martina.

Notes for email to Martina

1) Apology for not replying sooner.
2) Wrote new book. Sent to London publishing companies. Been offered contract.
3) Asked to make changes. More interesting for young people. Will work with editor.
4) Will pay me a lot of money. Can stop teaching & spend all my time writing.
5) Best part -- going to New York. First trip to USA. Meeting American editors & Hollywood film producers. Might make it into film.
6) Dinner together next week? New Italian restaurant in centre. Want to try?

UNIT 2
Reading and listening extension

1 READING

a Read the text and tick (✓) the correct answers.

1 Where might you see a text like this?
   - a ☐ in a book of short stories
   - b ☐ in a university textbook
   - c ☐ on a university website

2 What is the main purpose of this text?
   - a ☐ to explain how to program a robot dog
   - b ☐ to give people facts about the camp
   - c ☐ to persuade students to come to the camp

3 What is the main purpose of the student stories?
   - a ☐ to show that students can have fun while they learn
   - b ☐ to show that the camp can help your future career
   - c ☐ to show that the camp leaders are helpful

4 When did Dan and Kristen write their student stories?
   - a ☐ before the camp
   - b ☐ during the camp
   - c ☐ after the camp

b Read the text again and tick (✓) the correct answers.

Who ...	Dan	Kristen	Neither Dan nor Kristen
1 has been to the camp before?		✓	
2 says the camp is not the same as their normal education?			
3 felt unhappy at the beginning of the camp?			
4 is going to university soon?			
5 says they have improved their problem-solving skills?			
6 surprises people in their hometown with their knowledge of computers?			
7 was told about the camp at their school?			
8 prefers camp because they do not enjoy their normal school?			
9 has a busy social life in their hometown?			
10 mentions something they have been making at the camp?			

c Write a 'student story' for a course you are taking. Include the following:
   - how you felt about the course before you began
   - how you feel about the course now
   - what kind of things you have been doing (or did) on the course
   - why you think other people might enjoy the course.

COMPUTER CAMP

ABOUT
The first Computer Camp at the Central Scotland University (CSU) was in 2004. Since then, we have given more than 4,000 students a wonderful opportunity to improve their knowledge of computers and computer languages. The camp is for any student aged between 14 and 18 who wants to learn and have lots of fun at the same time.

STUDENT STORIES
Dan Austin from Glasgow, 15

This is my first time, so I didn't know what to expect. I've been having a really amazing time though and I really want to come back again. It's completely different from school and that's something I really like about the camp.

I've always got the highest marks in everything at my high school, and especially in maths. It was my maths teacher who told me about the camp. She persuaded my dad that it could help me get a career in computers. I suppose that must be true and I'm pretty sure that's why my dad let me come here, but for me I just enjoy it.

This week, I've been working on a program that can control the lights in a building. It's been really cool and I love working with kids who are just like me.

Kristen Berg from Aberdeen, 18

I've been coming to the CSU Computer Camp since I was 13 so this is my fifth time here. There's no doubt about it – this is one of the coolest things you can do in the summer holidays.

A lot of people back in Aberdeen are really surprised that I know so much about computers. They don't expect me to know anything about them because I'm a girl with long blonde hair and I love music, dancing and going out with friends. Every camp has been great and I've learned so much here. In fact, I'm starting a degree in Computer Science this October in Edinburgh.

2 LISTENING

a ▶️**2.5** Listen to part of a job interview. Put the topics from the interview in the order that you hear them.

- [ ] a practical skill someone has learned at work
- [ ] high school education
- [ ] an ability the employers think is useful
- [ ] work experience
- [ ] a qualification from university
- [ ] the place where one speaker was born
- [1] how the interview will be organised

b Listen to the interview again and tick (✓) the correct answers.

1 Carlos came to the interview …
  a ☐ by car.   b ☐ by plane.   c ✓ by train.
2 How old is Carlos?
  a ☐ 23   b ☐ 24   c ☐ 25
3 Where did Carlos study Computer Science?
  a ☐ in Spain   b ☐ in the UK   c ☐ in the US
4 How many languages does Carlos speak?
  a ☐ 2   b ☐ 3   c ☐ 4
5 When Carlos says he is 'a people person' he means that …
  a ☐ he can work with other people easily.
  b ☐ he has a specialist knowledge of people.
  c ☐ his family come from different countries.
6 What does Carlos do in his current job?
  a ☐ He creates apps for mobile phones.
  b ☐ He sells mobile phones.
  c ☐ He teaches computer languages.

c Look at the job advert below. Write a conversation between two people. Person A is interviewing Person B for the job of team leader. Use these questions to help you:

- Can you tell us about yourself? (name, age, work/study)
- What experience do you have that would be helpful for this job?
- Why do you think you would be a good team leader? (Person B gives reasons)

TEAM LEADER FOR INTERNATIONAL YOUTH SUMMER CAMP

Every year, the Central Scotland University (CSU) provides an International Youth Summer Camp for 600 children aged 12–14 from countries all around the world. The purpose of the camp is to:
- develop self-confidence and creative thinking
- teach problem-solving skills
- give opportunities to practice practical skills with technology
- let them have fun!

We are looking for people to be team leaders. Team leaders must:
- speak English and at least one other language
- have a positive attitude to work
- have knowledge about a sport, a skill or a hobby that will help students learn self-confidence, creative thinking, problem-solving or practical skills.

⊙ Review and extension

1 GRAMMAR

Correct the sentences. Use contractions where possible.

1 Did you ever go to Australia?
  Have you ever been to Australia?
2 I can't talk to Julia because she's spoken on the phone all day.
3 I've been to Portugal on holiday three years ago.
4 I've been knowing Jack for about five years.
5 His train was late this morning so he just arrived.
6 Last night she has gone to the party with her sister.
7 He works as a taxi driver since 2008.
8 She's got red eyes because she's cried.

2 VOCABULARY

Correct the sentences.

1 She's the manager of a game of five sales representatives.
  She's the manager of a team of five sales representatives.
2 Please turn out your phones as the film is about to start.
3 Can you give me your password so I can connect to Internet?
4 I've got a lot of experiences of managing people.
5 My brother just sent me a text massage to say he'll be late.
6 Sarah applied the job at the hospital but she didn't get it.
7 The English keyboard is different to the one in my language so I keep making mistakes when I press.
8 My brother has just got a new work with a large bank in London.

3 WORDPOWER *look*

Underline the correct words to complete the sentences.

1 I think we're lost. Let's look *after / at / out* the map so we can see where we are.
2 I looked *after / at / up* my friend's dog while she was away on holiday last week.
3 Can I help you? Yes, we're looking *after / for / out* a hotel.
4 Why don't you look *at / out / up* the phone number of the restaurant on the Internet?
5 I'm really looking *after / for / forward* to meeting you.
6 Shall we look *after / around / out* the old town to see if there are any nice places to eat?
7 Look *at / for / out!* There's an old lady crossing the road!

⊙ REVIEW YOUR PROGRESS

Look again at Review your progress on p.30 of the Student's Book. How well can you do these things now?
3 = very well   2 = well   1 = not so well

I CAN …

talk about experiences of work and training	☐
talk about technology	☐
make and respond to suggestions	☐
write an email giving news.	☐

3A I was working at a café when we met

1 GRAMMAR Narrative tenses

a Underline the correct words to complete the sentences.

1 By the time we *were getting* / *had got* / *got* to the park, it *had started* / *started* / *was starting* snowing heavily so we *were making* / *made* / *had made* a snowman.

2 While he *cleaned* / *had cleaned* / *was cleaning* the window above the door, he *had fallen* / *fell* / *was falling* off the chair and *broke* / *was breaking* / *had broken* his leg.

3 By the time it *stopped* / *had stopped* / *was stopping* raining, it *was* / *was being* / *had been* too late to go to the beach.

4 When the two police officers *were ringing* / *rang* / *had rung* my doorbell, I *was having* / *had* / *had had* dinner.

5 Barbara *was meeting* / *met* / *had met* him in 2010 while she *was working* / *worked* / *had worked* in Berlin.

6 When I *was seeing* / *had seen* / *saw* Mario yesterday, he *looked* / *was looking* / *had looked* sad because his pet rabbit *escaped* / *had escaped* / *was escaping* the day before.

7 They *talked* / *were talking* / *had talked* about the accident when the ambulance *had arrived* / *was arriving* / *arrived*.

b Complete the sentences with the past simple, the past continuous or the past perfect forms of the verbs in brackets.

1 He ____met____ (meet) his girlfriend while they _____ (study) together at Oxford University.

2 We _____ (leave) Barcelona on Monday morning and by Wednesday evening we _____ (cycle) 275 kilometres.

3 By the time the police _____ (arrive), the bank robbers _____ (escape) in their car.

4 This morning she _____ (ride) her bike around the lake and _____ (take) photos of the birds.

5 She _____ (hear) the fireworks while she _____ (watch) a film on TV.

6 The car _____ (crash) into the tree while they _____ (cross) the road.

7 The restaurant _____ (close) by the time we _____ (get) there.

8 Ibrahim _____ (call) me while he _____ (wait) for his flight.

2 VOCABULARY Relationships

a Match 1–6 with a–f to make sentences and questions.

1 [d] I've always had a good
2 [ ] They come from the same
3 [ ] I think that he's really funny – he's got a great
4 [ ] They have a lot of shared
5 [ ] Who do you get
6 [ ] I have quite a few things

a on best with – your brother or your sister?
b in common with Jack. For example, we both like rap music
c background. Both of their families were farmers in Wales.
d relationship with both of my parents.
e interests. They're both mad about football and photography
f sense of humour even when things go wrong.

b Complete the sentences with the words in the box.

relatives ~~touch~~ friendship
support stranger humour

1 It's easy to keep in ____touch____ with your family when you go on a business trip – you can send emails and texts and talk to them via Skype.

2 Our _____ is really important to us. We've known each other since we were five years old.

3 When he came back to his home town, he felt like a complete _____. All of his friends had moved to London so he didn't know anyone.

4 Louise gave me a lot of _____ when I got divorced. She really helped me during a very difficult time in my life.

5 I have some _____ in both Montreal and Quebec because two of my uncles moved to Canada in the 1980s.

6 He's got a fantastic sense of _____. He's always telling us jokes and making us laugh.

3 PRONUNCIATION Linking

a ▶ 3.1 Listen to the sentences. Underline the linked words where one word ends in a consonant sound and the next word starts with a vowel sound.

1 Mark and Tania got to know each other when they worked in Spain.
2 They've got lots of shared interests.
3 He gets on very well with his aunt.
4 I'm not very good at keeping in touch with old friends.
5 What does she have in common with her American cousin

3B We used to get together every year

1 GRAMMAR *used to, usually*

a <u>Underline</u> the correct words to complete the sentences.

1 Our family *usually get together* / *used to get together* on Sundays. It's nice to keep in touch with everyone.
2 These days I *usually walk* / *used to walk* to work – it's much healthier.
3 When I was seven, my parents *usually send* / *used to send* me to stay with my grandparents in Scotland for six weeks.
4 *Do you usually get* / *Did you used to get* on well with your teachers when you were at primary school?
5 She *doesn't usually like* / *didn't use to like* tea or coffee when she was little.
6 When I was a little girl I *usually hang out* / *used to hang out* with my cousin and her friends a lot.
7 As I was an only child, I *didn't use to have* / *don't usually have* a brother or sister to play with during the holidays.
8 *Did you used to take* / *Do you usually take* the bus to work when it rains?

b Complete the article with the verbs in the box and the correct form of *used to* or the present simple.

drive   live   go   sit   eat

Before Jason won the lottery two years ago, he ¹ _used to live_ in a small flat next to the train station. Now he ² _____ in an enormous house with a swimming pool and a tennis court. Jason ³ _____ a 15-year-old car but these days he ⁴ _____ a brand new Ferrari. Before winning the lottery he hardly ever ⁵ _____ on holiday but nowadays he usually ⁶ _____ on holiday to places like Bali or the Caribbean. On hot summer days Jason ⁷ _____ in the park but these days he usually ⁸ _____ by the swimming pool in his enormous garden. When Jason didn't have much money he ⁹ _____ in restaurants very often but now he usually ¹⁰ _____ in expensive restaurants three or four times a week.

2 VOCABULARY Family

a Complete the sentences with the words in the box.

niece   childhood   ~~elder~~   only
nephew   eldest   middle   generations

1 Pauline is my _____elder_____ sister. She was born two years before me.
2 My brother's son's birthday is next week. I've just bought him a card that says, 'Happy birthday, _____!'
3 I had a very happy _____. My parents spent a lot of time with us and we used to laugh all the time.
4 Jane's two years older than me and Joe's one year younger so I'm the _____ child.
5 It wasn't much fun being an _____ child. I never had any brothers or sisters to play with.
6 I've got two brothers and Nick is the _____. He's 26, Mike is 20 and I'm 23.
7 My sister's just had a new baby girl, so now I've got a _____.
8 There will be four _____ of our family at the wedding! My great-grandfather will be there too!

3 VOCABULARY Multi-word verbs

a Match 1–8 with a–h to make sentences.

1 ☐f When I was a teenager I used to hang
2 ☐ John's got a great sense of humour. I think he takes
3 ☐ After I left home, my parents started to grow
4 ☐ In *The Jungle Book*, Mowgli was brought
5 ☐ When Megan felt lonely she used to ring
6 ☐ I've got an identical twin and some people have always mixed us
7 ☐ All the students from my old class get
8 ☐ Most people think that I'm English, but in fact I grew

a up her mother for a chat.
b up by a family of wolves. It's an incredible story.
c up in Ireland and then came to live in London after university.
d together every two or three years for a reunion party.
e after his grandad, who was always telling jokes.
f out with my elder brother and his friends.
g apart and two years later they got divorced.
h up. They can't tell the difference between us.

3C Everyday English
You won't believe what I did!

1 USEFUL LANGUAGE
Telling a story

a Complete the sentences with the words in the box.

| matters turned anyway end |
| won't guess ~~thing~~ funny |

1 The best ___thing___ is that my new flat is air conditioned.
2 _____, we still hadn't found a hotel for my grandparents.
3 In the _____, we bought him a computer game.
4 It _____ out that he had never played golf in his life.
5 You'll never _____ what Sarah said to David.
6 The _____ thing was that he didn't know she was joking.
7 You _____ believe what he bought her for her birthday. A snake!
8 To make _____ worse, the water was too cold to have a shower.

b ▶ 3.2 Listen and check.

c Put the words in the correct order to make sentences.

1 guess / you'll / happened / the / what / party / never / at .
   <u>You'll never guess what happened at the party.</u>
2 best / got / pool / thing / that / the / it's / swimming / a / is .
   _____
3 Maggie / we still / find / had / to / a / anyway, / for / present .
   _____
4 heavily / worse, / make / raining / to / it / matters / started .
   _____
5 did / you / believe / Saturday / I / on / what / won't .
   _____
6 funny / the / what / realise / thing / was / she / that / didn't / happened / had .
   _____
7 in / us / end, / the / he / the / to drive / to / station / agreed .
   _____
8 ticket / it / out / had / that / turned / train / she / her / lost .
   _____

d ▶ 3.3 Listen and check.

2 PRONUNCIATION
Stress in word groups

a ▶ 3.4 Listen to the sentences and <u>underline</u> the words before the speakers pause.

1 But, <u>anyway</u>, the train was still at the <u>station</u> and we got on just as the doors were closing.
2 In the end, we went to a little restaurant near the station, where we had a lovely meal.
3 To make matters worse, the waiter dropped the bottle of wine and it ruined my new white dress.
4 On top of that, when she eventually got to the airport they told her that her flight was nearly two hours late.
5 Anyway, in the end I found a lovely flat in the centre, and the best thing is that it's only 800 euros a month!

b Listen to the sentences again and <u>underline</u> the stressed syllables.

1 But, <u>a</u>nyway, the train was still at the <u>sta</u>tion and we got on just as the doors were <u>clos</u>ing.
2 In the end, we went to a little restaurant near the station, where we had a lovely meal.
3 To make matters worse, the waiter dropped the bottle of wine and it ruined my new white dress.
4 On top of that, when she eventually got to the airport they told her that her flight was nearly two hours late.
5 Anyway, in the end I found a lovely flat in the centre, and the best thing is that it's only eight hundred euros a month!

1 READING

a Read the email and tick (✓) the correct answer.

- a ☐ Jack played professional football in the 1960s.
- b ☐ Jack played for Newcastle United for five years.
- c ☐ Jack joined Newcastle United in 1953.
- d ☐ Jack scored 100 goals for the factory team.

b Read the email again. Are the sentences true or false?

1. Paolo and Carla's uncle used to be a professional footballer.
2. When Jack was 16 he played for Newcastle United.
3. Jack was still playing professional football in the 1960s.
4. Jack and Giulia got married two years after they met.
5. Jack and Giulia died in 1992.

2 WRITING SKILLS Describing time

a Match 1–6 with a–f to make sentences.

1. ☐f☐ She lived in Buenos Aires for
2. ☐ He continued studying until he was 22. Meanwhile,
3. ☐ He visited the Grand Canyon during
4. ☐ Uncle Julian was a major in the army from 1986
5. ☐ She worked as a receptionist over
6. ☐ My parents met a long time ago while

a his first business trip to the USA.
b his twin brother was working in the family's shoe factory.
c they were both teaching English in Indonesia.
d the summer holidays when it was particularly busy.
e until his retirement a few years ago.
f seven years before moving to England.

3 WRITING

a Read the notes. Imagine your grandfather was James Cooper. Write his biography.

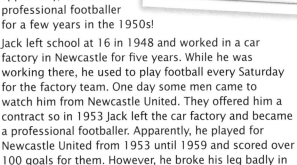

⊙ Mail

Hi Carla

I've been talking to Dad about our family history and I've found out some interesting things about his brother Giacomo, our Uncle Jack. Well, apparently, he was a professional footballer for a few years in the 1950s!

Jack left school at 16 in 1948 and worked in a car factory in Newcastle for five years. While he was working there, he used to play football every Saturday for the factory team. One day some men came to watch him from Newcastle United. They offered him a contract so in 1953 Jack left the car factory and became a professional footballer. Apparently, he played for Newcastle United from 1953 until 1959 and scored over 100 goals for them. However, he broke his leg badly in 1959 and had to give up playing professional football.

After that, he got a job as a sports teacher at a local secondary school and that's where he met his wife, Auntie Giulia. She was an Art teacher. They fell in love and got married two years later, in 1961. Our cousins Luigi and Anna were born in 1962 and 1964. As you know, we left Great Britain and came to live here in Australia in 1965, so it was quite difficult for Dad and Uncle Jack to keep in touch after that.

Meanwhile, in 1969 Uncle Jack and Auntie Giulia opened an Italian restaurant called La Forchetta in the centre of Newcastle. During the 1970s and 1980s this was the most popular Italian restaurant in Newcastle. Sadly, in 1992 Uncle Jack was killed in a car crash and Auntie Giulia decided to sell the restaurant.

When I travel to the UK on business later this year, I'm planning to meet our cousins, Luigi and Anna.

Hope to see you soon

Paolo

Notes for biography of James Cooper (Grandad)

Introduction: James Cooper (Grandad). My sister and I very fond of him. Remember lunch with grandparents every Sunday when young. Always made us laugh – lots of jokes and funny stories.

Life story:
1928 Born London. Very happy childhood. 1 brother & 2 sisters.
1936 Family moved to Montreal. Stayed there 10 years. Spoke English and French.
1946–1952 Studied medicine at Cambridge University, UK.
1952 Graduated from Cambridge.
1953–1962 Worked in different hospitals in UK.
1962–1975 Job in hospital in San Francisco. Met Elspeth Clark (Grandma).
1964 Married Elspeth.
1965 My mother born. No other children.
1975–1980 Job in Johannesburg, South Africa. Friendship with famous heart surgeon Christiaan Barnard.
1988 Retired aged 60.
2000 Died aged 72. Miss him very much.

UNIT 3
Reading and listening extension

1 READING

a Read the text and tick (✓) the correct answers.

1 This text comes from …
  a ☐ a newspaper article.
  b ☐ a novel.
  c ☐ an essay.

2 Which of these adjectives best describes the text?
  a ☐ amusing   b ☐ romantic   c ☐ strange

3 What is the best way to describe what happens in this text?
  a ☐ A student cannot complete an essay because of a noise outside her room.
  b ☐ A student is trying to complete an essay when something unusual happens.
  c ☐ A student is waiting for her friends to ring her up but they come to her house instead.

4 In the text, what is compared to 'a busy teacher'?
  a ☐ a clock   b ☐ a computer   c ☐ a drawer

5 In the text, what is compared to 'a dog's nose'?
  a ☐ the curtains   b ☐ the rain   c ☐ the streets

b The order of the events in the story is different from the order that the events happened. Read the text again and put the events in the order they happened.

☐ Jen started writing her essay.
☐ It stopped raining.
☐ Jen had a big shock.
☐ A voice called Jen's name.
1 It started raining.
☐ Jen heard a noise outside.
☐ The group hid from Jen.
☐ Jen turned her computer on.

c Write a short story that begins with this sentence:
I had just arrived at the cinema when Larissa called.

Jen sighed heavily. She hadn't done anything for at least ten minutes. She looked at the clock and the clock looked back at her. It was like a busy teacher: 'tick', 'tick', 'tick' … It ticked every second and the seconds became minutes. Jen sighed again, even more heavily this time.

'You're no friend of mine,' she said, picking up the noisy clock. She walked to the other side of her bedroom, opened a drawer, threw the clock in and closed it again. Jen went back to her computer to do some more sighing. None of her friends were online and she had at least another 500 words to write.

Suddenly, there was a noise from outside. Jen went over to the window, opened the curtains just a centimetre and put one eye very carefully to the gap. It had been raining that day and the streets were as cold, black and wet as a dog's nose. She couldn't see very clearly, but she could hear them.

There was a group of maybe seven or eight figures all hanging out together. She checked her phone – no one had sent her a text in the last five minutes. She looked at the computer – everyone she knew was still offline. So who were they?

The laughing and shouting from outside had become much louder so Jen went to the curtains for another look. As soon as she opened the curtains, everything went quiet.

'That's strange,' she thought. The whole group had disappeared. She listened more carefully but there was only silence.

'JEN! JEN!! WE CAN *SEE* YOU, JEN!!!' eight voices shouted at once.

There was a feeling like someone had poured a glass of ice-water into her stomach and suddenly she was jumping away from the curtains, her hand over her mouth.

'JEEEeennnn …' came a single voice, 'JEEEeennnn …'

Jen froze. Whose voice was it? Was it someone she knew? A stranger? Who could it be? There was only one way to find out …

2 LISTENING

a ▶ **3.5** Listen to part of a conversation between two students at a university. Are the sentences true or false?

1 Education is the main topic of the conversation.
2 The conversation is a friendly chat.
3 One of the speakers is from Africa.
4 The speakers have not met before.
5 One speaker describes his/her family.
6 Relationships are the main topic of the conversation.
7 The conversation is an interview.
8 One speaker is a professional sportsperson.

b Listen to the conversation again and tick (✓) the correct answers

1 What is Ben studying at university?
  a ☐ Economics
  b ☐ Physics
  c ☐ Politics

2 How old is Ben?
  a ☐ 24
  b ☐ 28
  c ☐ 32

3 Rosie is surprised that Ben …
  a ☐ has a girlfriend.
  b ☐ is already married.
  c ☐ is not in a relationship.

4 How many sisters does Ben have?
  a ☐ 3
  b ☐ 5
  c ☐ 6

5 Ben believes he is confident because …
  a ☐ he has always been good at sport.
  b ☐ his family looked after him.
  c ☐ there are so many women in his family.

6 Why did Ben not like Zippy when they first met?
  a ☐ Because Zippy did not understand Ben's sense of humour.
  b ☐ Because Zippy was a better football player than Ben.
  c ☐ Because Zippy's sister had an argument with Ben.

c Write a conversation between two people discussing family and friendship. Use these questions to help you:
• How would you describe your childhood?
• Do you keep in touch with friends you made at school?
• How important is a sense of humour in friendship?
• What other things are important in a good friendship?

◉ Review and extension

1 GRAMMAR

Correct the sentences.

1 He phoned me while I got ready to go out.
   He phoned me while I was getting ready to go out.
2 I use to have long hair when I was a little girl.
3 He played football when he fell over and hurt his ankle.
4 When he got to his house he was angry because someone broke his window.
5 I got to the station five minutes late this morning and, unfortunately, my normal train already left.
6 After the film we were going to the café for a drink.
7 Did you used to play football when you were at school?
8 I didn't used to like English when I was at school.

2 VOCABULARY

Correct the sentences.

1 I've never had a very good relation with my sister.
   I've never had a very good relationship with my sister.
2 Joanne's mother died when she was three so she was grown up by her grandparents.
3 I got knowing Jasmine really well when we went travelling around South America together.
4 All my relatives met together at my dad's birthday party.
5 I don't have any brothers or sisters so I'm a lonely child.
6 She doesn't go on very well with her two brothers.
7 We share a lot of the same interestings, for example literature.
8 My little brother's very calm and patient, so he looks after his mother because she's like that too.

3 WORDPOWER *have*

Complete the sentences with the words in the box.

idea ~~lesson~~ go look time lunch

1 My son has a piano ___lesson___ every Monday after school.
2 We had a great _____ at Debbie's party.
3 I felt really hungry so I had _____ at 12 o'clock.
4 I had no _____ they had got divorced.
5 Are those your holiday photos? Can I have a _____?
6 Do you want to have a _____ on my skateboard?

⟳ REVIEW YOUR PROGRESS

Look again at Review your progress on p.42 of the Student's Book. How well can you do these things now?
3 = very well   2 = well   1 = not so well

I CAN ...

talk about a friendship	☐
talk about families	☐
tell a story	☐
write about someone's life.	☐

4A I could sing quite well when I was younger

1 GRAMMAR
Modals and phrases of ability

a <u>Underline</u> the correct words to complete the sentences.

1 He *wasn't able to* / *won't be able to* / <u>*hasn't been able to*</u> practise with the band since he started his new job.
2 Your sister speaks English really well. *Could you* / *Can you* / *Have you been able to* speak it as well as her?
3 By the time he was seven, *he can* / *he could* / *he's been able to* speak four languages fluently.
4 The banks are all closed now, but, don't worry; *you'll be able to* / *you could* / *you were able to* change some money tomorrow morning.
5 He missed the last bus but, fortunately, he *could* / *can* / *was able to* find a taxi to take him back to the hotel.
6 I *can't* / *couldn't* / *haven't been able to* find where your street was, so in the end I asked a policeman.
7 Before she goes abroad on holiday, she tries to learn some of the language, as she likes *being able to* / *can* / *will be able to* say a few words to the people she meets.
8 She looked everywhere in her apartment but she *can't* / *won't be able to* / *didn't manage to* find her car keys.

b Match 1–6 with a–f to make sentences.

1 [b] Tomorrow the weather will definitely be better, so you
2 [ ] Even when he was a child, Pablo Picasso
3 [ ] I've
4 [ ] He spoke very slowly so we
5 [ ] I'm learning Greek because I want to
6 [ ] We looked everywhere but in the end, we didn't

a be able to speak to my wife's family in their language.
b will be able to go to the beach.
c were able to understand him easily.
d been able to ride a bike since I was three years old.
e manage to find a hotel room.
f could draw really well.

2 VOCABULARY Ability

a <u>Underline</u> the correct word to complete the sentences.

1 To run 20 marathons in less than a month was an incredible *success* / *achievement* / *attitude*.
2 She has the *ability* / *success* / *achievement* to learn languages very quickly.
3 Jenny has a really positive attitude *at* / *towards* / *to* her studies. She works really hard.
4 I am *brilliant* / *confident* / *determined* to get a grade A in the exam.
5 They were one of the most *successful* / *determined* / *confident* bands of the 1960s. They sold millions of records.
6 Unfortunately, he *succeeded in* / *achieved* / *gave up* studying languages when he was 14 so his English isn't very good.

b Complete the crossword puzzle.

										1	
²B	R	I	L	L	I	³A	N	T			
					4						
				⁵							
			⁶								
⁷											

→ Across

2 He was absolutely b<u>rilliant</u> at chess. He could beat his father when he was only seven.
4 Rafael Nadal is an extremely c_____ tennis player – he expects to win every game he plays.
5 He was easily the most s_____ manager in the history of this football club. He won the championship eight times.
6 Although she felt extremely tired, she was d_____ to finish the marathon so she continued running.
7 Roger Federer is probably the most t_____ tennis player of his generation.

↓ Down

1 He had a great sense of humour and he loved telling jokes. He always had the a_____ to make people laugh.
2 She was extremely b_____ – probably the most intelligent student I've ever taught.
3 In the 1960s, NASA's greatest a_____ was to land a spacecraft on the moon.

B Are you an introvert?

1 GRAMMAR Articles

a Complete the sentences with *a*, *an*, *the* or *Ø* (zero article).

1 On ____Ø____ Saturday we went to _____ best Chinese restaurant in _____ London.
2 Do you know if there's _____ bank near here where I can buy _____ dollars?
3 I don't go to _____ school on _____ Saturdays.
4 Sometimes it's difficult to find _____ doctor when you live in _____ countryside.
5 **A** I saw _____ Italian film on TV last night. It was called *Cinema Paradiso*.
   B Really? What did you think of _____ film?
6 I think _____ Spanish people are very friendly.
7 I eat _____ fish two or three times _____ week.
8 Venice is one of _____ most beautiful cities in _____ world.

b Correct the sentences.

1 He's working as translator in UK.
   He's working as a translator in the UK.
2 I usually go to gym three times the week.
   _____
3 Is there supermarket opposite a bus stop near your house?
   _____
4 She usually goes to the school on Number 75 bus.
   _____
5 I often listen to radio before I go to the bed.
   _____
6 The British pop groups are very popular in USA.
   _____
7 There isn't the underground station near my hotel, so I'll have to take taxi.
   _____
8 Usain Bolt was fastest man in world at Olympic Games in 2012.
   _____

2 VOCABULARY -ed/-ing adjectives

a Underline the correct adjectives to complete the sentences.

1 I watched a *fascinating* / *fascinated* documentary about tigers on TV last night.
2 I was so *boring* / *bored* during his lecture that I nearly fell asleep.
3 That was one of the most *terrifying* / *terrified* horror films I've ever seen.
4 I'm looking forward to doing nothing when I go on holiday next week. It's going to be so *relaxing* / *relaxed*.
5 The children were really *disappointing* / *disappointed* when Uncle Paul didn't bring them a present.
6 This cloudy, wet weather is so *depressing* / *depressed*. There hasn't been any sunshine for weeks!
7 I'm not really *interesting* / *interested* in modern art.
8 If you aren't completely *satisfying* / *satisfied* with the service, you shouldn't leave the waiter a tip.

3 VOCABULARY Personality adjectives

a Complete the sentences with the words in the box.

sensitive talkative introvert shy ~~active~~ serious extrovert sociable

1 Bill and Philip are really __*active*__. In their free time they always go running or swimming or they play football. They never seem to relax.
2 My brother's an _____. He likes spending time with other people and he's very good at making new friends.
3 Sarah's extremely _____. You have to be very careful with what you say to her, as she gets upset very easily.
4 Amanda's rather _____. She doesn't like meeting new people and she hates going to parties where she doesn't know anyone.
5 I think Joe's very _____. He has a lot of friends and he really enjoys meeting new people.
6 My sister is so _____. She often chats to her friends on the phone for hours!
7 Charles has very few friends and spends most of his time by himself. I think he's an _____.
8 James is a _____ student. He works very hard all the time and he rarely goes out with friends.

4C Everyday English
Do you need a hand?

1 USEFUL LANGUAGE Question tags

a Match 1–9 with a–i to make questions.

1 [h] You don't smoke any more,
2 ☐ It's a lovely day today,
3 ☐ Tom isn't going to ask her to marry him,
4 ☐ You haven't been waiting long for me,
5 ☐ She'd already bought him a present,
6 ☐ They'll phone us when they get to the airport,
7 ☐ The twins both got good grades in their exams,
8 ☐ Andrew speaks five languages fluently,
9 ☐ You don't want any rice, Jim,

a doesn't he?
b didn't they?
c have you?
d won't they?
e isn't it?
f is he?
g hadn't she?
h do you?
i do you?

b ▶ 4.1 Listen and check.

2 CONVERSATION SKILLS
Offering and asking for help

a Complete the exchanges with the words in the box.

favour   need   return   could   how
something   ask   ~~wondered~~   help   hand

1 **A** I ___wondered___ if you could do me a favour?
  B Sure, _____ can I help you?
  A Do you think you _____ cut the grass in my garden for me?
  B Yes, of course. No problem.

2 **A** I've got a lot of things to get ready for the party tomorrow night.
  B Is there _____ I can do?
  A Yes, there is, actually. Can you give me a _____ with the shopping?
  B Yes, that's fine. Could I ask you a favour in _____?
  A Go ahead!
  B Could you lend me your black trousers for tomorrow?
  A No problem. I'll just get them for you.

3 **A** Could I ask you a _____, Ben?
  B Of course, what do you _____?
  A Could you _____ me move my desk into the other office?
  B Actually, I've got a bad back. Can you _____ someone else?

b ▶ 4.2 Listen and check.

3 PRONUNCIATION
Intonation in question tags

a ▶ 4.3 Listen to the sentences. Does the intonation go up ↗ or down ↘? Tick (✓) the correct answer.

	↗	↘
1 You've been to Cairo before, haven't you?	✓	☐
2 Jack's really good at tennis, isn't he?	☐	☐
3 They've got four children, haven't they?	☐	☐
4 This is the best beach in Thailand, isn't it?	☐	☐
5 You're glad you left London, aren't you?	☐	☐
6 You didn't go to Canada last year, did you?	☐	☐

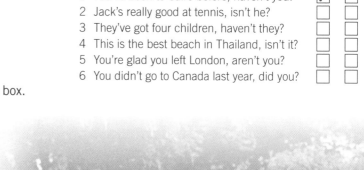

Skills for Writing
No experience needed

1 READING

a Read both adverts and tick (✓) the correct answer.

1 If you want to go on the adventure holiday in the Atlas Mountains, you …
   a ☐ have to be good at riding camels.
   b ☐ have to be under 30.
   c ☐ need to have a good bike.
   d ☐ mustn't be an introvert or a shy person.

2 If you want to be a volunteer English teacher, you should …
   a ☐ have a lot of experience of teaching.
   b ☐ be able to work well with children.
   c ☐ be able to speak another language very well.
   d ☐ have your own car.

Trekking in the Atlas Mountains

We're looking for three or four people to join us on a 2-week adventure holiday in Morocco. We're meeting up in Marrakech on 27 April and spending 10 days walking and camping in the Atlas Mountains.

We're planning to climb Mount Toubkal, the highest mountain in North Africa, visit Berber villages and travel through a section of the Sahara Desert. We're also planning to go horse-riding and mountain-biking and we may also get the chance to ride a few camels! We'll spend the last 2–3 days exploring the fabulous city of Marrakech.

Ideally, you should be in your twenties or thirties with an outgoing personality and a sense of adventure. You should be good at getting on well with people and making friends easily. You should be very fit and have some experience of walking with a backpack in mountainous areas.

If this sounds like the trip for you, email us at the address below and we'll get back to you as soon as possible.

Jake, Suzie and Gary

Volunteer English teachers needed – 6 hours a week

Duties include teaching English to schoolchildren with a low level of English in local primary schools and to adults from all over the world that have come to work in the UK.

No qualifications or previous teaching experience needed. Volunteers will be required to attend a training programme. Candidates should be enthusiastic and outgoing and be good at working with children and adults. Candidates should be educated to degree level, have good English language skills and some experience of learning a foreign language.

Please complete the attached online application form. One of our coordinators will get in touch with you to discuss potential opportunities. Reasonable travel expenses reimbursed.

b Read the adverts again. Are the sentences true or false?

1 There will be eight people in the group that goes on the holiday to the Atlas Mountains.
2 They aren't planning to go walking in the mountains every day of the trip.
3 The people who go on this trip don't need to have any previous experience of walking in mountains.
4 The adults that are learning English come from lots of different countries.
5 New teachers don't need to receive any training.
6 It is better if new teachers have previously studied another language.

2 WRITING SKILLS
The language of adverts

a Match sentences 1–8 with the reduced expressions a–h.

1 [g] Candidates don't need to pay for a place to stay.
2 ☐ Candidates must be able to drive a car.
3 ☐ We will need to see your references from your previous jobs.
4 ☐ We're looking for someone with a university degree.
5 ☐ It doesn't matter if you've never done this job before.
6 ☐ The candidate needs to have previous classroom experience.
7 ☐ Candidates should be able to speak French.
8 ☐ We will train the successful applicant to do the job.

3 WRITING

a Read the notes. Write an advert for summer camp coaches.

Notes for summer camp coaches advert

Camp for children 5--12 years.

Duties: Organise indoor/outdoor activities. Get kids ready in morning. Help at meal & bed times. Entertain during free time.

Person requirements: Energetic, enthusiastic, sense of adventure, sense of humour & positive attitude. Good at sports & art, etc. Must love working with children & work well with others in a team. 18 or over. University students/graduates preferred.

No experience required. Two-day training course.

Online application form & CV to Human Resources Dept. HRD will contact applicants for interviews.

a No previous experience needed.
b University graduate preferred.
c Teaching experience required.
d Full training programme provided.
e French-speaker preferred.
f Good references required.
g Accommodation provided.
h Driving licence required.

UNIT 4
Reading and listening extension

1 READING

a Read the text and tick (✓) the correct answers.

1 Where might you usually see this kind of text?
 a ☐ in a newspaper
 b ☐ in an email from a friend
 c ☐ on the back of a book

2 According to the reviewer, 'self-help' books …
 a ☐ are usually very expensive
 b ☐ have a large number of readers
 c ☐ help readers earn more money

3 Where did Burkeman go to collect information for the book?
 a ☐ capital cities in Europe
 b ☐ countries in North and South America
 c ☐ many different places

4 The reviewer enjoys a description of …
 a ☐ a family party
 b ☐ a funeral in a small town
 c ☐ a traditional festival

b Read the text again. Are the sentences true or false?

1 The phrase 'worth their weight in gold' in the first paragraph means 'valuable'.

2 Burkeman's book *The Antidote* is a typical example of a 'self-help' book.

3 Burkeman did not expect to find happiness in some of the places he visited.

4 Burkeman discovers that life is more difficult for people when they have a lot of money.

5 Burkeman says we cannot understand happiness unless we also have bad experiences.

6 People are often happy and enjoy themselves during the Day of the Dead.

7 Although there are some good parts, the reviewer does not recommend this book.

c Write a review of a non-fiction book you have enjoyed reading. Include the following:

- the name of the author and the title of the book
- a paragraph describing the general topic of the book
- a paragraph describing the main ideas in the book
- a paragraph describing the best part(s) of the book
- a recommendation which explains why other people should read the book.

BOOK Reviews

THE ANTIDOTE: HAPPINESS FOR PEOPLE WHO CAN'T STAND POSITIVE THINKING

by Oliver Burkeman

Is your life disappointing? Does that make you feel depressed? If you answered 'yes' to those two questions, what can you do to find happiness? The answers to these questions can be worth their weight in gold – last year, people spent almost $11 billion on 'self-help' books. These books promise to make us more confident, more sociable and more successful. They tell us that all we really need to find love and achieve our goals is a positive attitude.

If you are amused by promises like these, then Oliver Burkeman's book *The Antidote* might just be for you. Burkeman has travelled the world in search of happiness and he has found it in some very unusual places. For example, he meets poor people in Africa who seem to be happier than some wealthy people he knows in London. For Burkeman, this shows us that people who do not own very much cannot worry about losing it. In other words, having a lot of things can add a lot of stress to our lives. Of course he is not saying that poor people in Africa have an easy life. Instead, Burkeman uses this example to talk about 'negative paths'.

A 'negative path' is important for a satisfying life. He suggests that we need to remind ourselves that bad things happen and that we should learn to live with them. True happiness – if it exists – must include both positive and negative experiences. A complete life should be one that knows hate as well as love and illness as well as health.

In my favourite part of the book, Burkeman takes us to a small village in Mexico on the Day of the Dead. The Day of the Dead is a festival that celebrates everyone who has died. However, it is not a sad festival at all, but a colourful party for friends and family. According to Burkeman, we need events like this to remember why we should be happy more often. *The Antidote* is an interesting book that has the ability to make you feel that happiness really is possible.

2 LISTENING

a ▶ **4.4** Listen to an expert in advertising tell a story during a talk to university students and tick (✓) the correct answers.

1 Where did the story take place?
  a ☐ in England b ☐ in Germany c ☐ in Russia

2 Why did Frederick want people to start eating potatoes?
  a ☐ because they were cheap and easy to grow
  b ☐ because they were the solution to a problem
  c ☐ because they were very popular with the people

3 Frederick was surprised that the people …
  a ☐ did not know how to grow potatoes.
  b ☐ gave the potatoes to their animals.
  c ☐ said they could not eat the potatoes.

4 According to the speaker, the story can teach us something about …
  a ☐ food. b ☐ history. c ☐ psychology.

b Listen again and correct the information in the sentences. Use the words in the box to help you. You do not need all the words.

---
animal be successful bread business hungry
meat psychology soldier steal ~~talented~~

---

1 Frederick II is sometimes called Frederick the Great because he was so tall.
  Frederick II is sometimes called Frederick the Great
  because he was so talented.

2 Cheese was the most important part of most people's diet.
  _____

3 Frederick thought that if people had potatoes, they would not be angry any more.
  _____

4 People in Kolberg said their children could not eat potatoes.
  _____

5 People understood that potatoes were valuable when they saw the gates around Frederick's garden.
  _____

6 People began eating potatoes from Frederick's garden.
  _____

7 Frederick's plan did not work.
  _____

8 Frederick's plan was an example of good farming.
  _____

c Think of a story about a famous person or event in your country. Use these questions to make notes:

• Does the story teach a lesson?
  (For example, can the story help people become more patient / more confident / healthier?)
• Who are the main characters in the story?
• What happens?

Write the story.

◉ Review and extension

1 GRAMMAR

Correct the sentences.

1 I've could speak English since I was seven years old.
  I've been able to speak English since I was seven years old.
2 When she goes to cinema she doesn't like seeing the horror films.
3 Will you can help me with my Maths homework this evening?
4 I love watching the documentaries about the whales.
5 She would like to can play the piano as well as her sister.
6 He usually gets to the work at about 8.30 in summer.
7 We weren't able find the restaurant so we went to the pizzeria instead.
8 It's one of best shopping websites on Internet.

2 VOCABULARY

Correct the sentences.

1 He has very positive attitude towards his studies.
  He has a very positive attitude towards his studies.
2 We had a very relax holiday in the South of France.
3 The film was so bored that I nearly fell asleep.
4 My uncle was a very succesful businessman in the 1960s.
5 My sister doesn't want to watch the match because she isn't very interesting in sport.
6 I thought that documentary about the environment was rather depressed.

3 WORDPOWER *so and such*

Complete the sentences with the words in the box.

---
so far such ~~such a~~ and so on so tired or so

---

1 He's __such a__ brilliant musician!
2 He's been fishing for six hours and _____ he hasn't caught any fish.
3 It's a short book – no more than 100 pages _____.
4 To make a cake you'll need all the usual things – sugar, flour, butter _____.
5 It will be _____ fun at the party on Saturday, won't it?
6 I was _____ that I fell asleep on the train.

◗ REVIEW YOUR PROGRESS

Look again at Review your progress on p.54 of the Student's Book. How well can you do these things now?
3 = very well   2 = well   1 = not so well

I CAN …

describe people and their abilities	☐
describe feelings	☐
offer and ask for help	☐
write an informal online advert.	☐

5A People will care more about the environment

1 GRAMMAR Future forms

a Match 1–8 with a–h to make sentences and questions.

1 [f] Jack really hates his job, so he's going to
2 [ ] Don't worry – this year I promise I won't
3 [ ] At 1 o'clock I'm
4 [ ] Brian's been studying very hard, so I'm sure he
5 [ ] I probably won't
6 [ ] What a lovely day! Shall we
7 [ ] Look at those dark clouds. I think it's
8 [ ] Your train doesn't get here until 11.30, so shall I

a meeting Susie for lunch at Café Classic.
b 'll get good grades in his exams.
c meet you at the station in my car?
d going to rain. Let's stay inside.
e go to the beach this afternoon?
f start looking for a new one in September.
g forget your birthday!
h see her today, as she usually visits her grandparents on Sundays.

b Correct the sentences.

1 **A** Will we go out for a pizza tonight?
Shall we go out for a pizza tonight?
B Yes, good idea. I'm phoning the pizzeria to book a table.

2 **A** What time shall your brother arrive?

B This evening. I drive to the station to meet him at 6.30.

3 Hello, John. The traffic's really bad in the centre. We're being about 20 minutes late.

4 In my opinion the next president of the USA shall be a Republican.

5 Will I help you bring in the shopping from the car?

6 **A** What time shall you have your hair cut this afternoon?

B I've made an appointment for 3 o'clock.

7 I don't think Brazil is winning the football match tomorrow.

8 **A** What are Ricky's plans for the future?
B I don't know. Perhaps he's getting a job in that new hotel at the beach.

2 VOCABULARY Environmental issues

a Match 1–5 with a–e to make sentences.

1 [a] People should be able to recycle
2 [ ] Air pollution has seriously damaged
3 [ ] The environmental group are trying to prevent
4 [ ] Around 1,500 pandas survive
5 [ ] Environmental organisations are trying to save

a more than 50% of their household rubbish.
b the Siberian tiger from extinction.
c in the mountains of Western China.
d the destruction of the rainforest in Puerto Rico.
e the outside of the pyramids near Cairo.

b Complete the sentences with the words in the box.

wildlife   conservation   environmentally   pollution
climate   destroyed   ~~environment~~   endangered

1 We have to protect the _environment_ for future generations.
2 Scientists are very worried about _____ change.
3 The _____ caused by cars and lorries is affecting air quality in the city centre.
4 The hybrid car is the most _____ friendly car.
5 Large areas of the Amazon Rainforest are _____ by farmers every year.
6 The black rhino is an _____ species. There are very few animals left in the wild.
7 There is incredible _____ in Kenya, including lions, elephants and giraffes.
8 I'm working on a _____ project at the moment to protect and preserve rare plants.

3 PRONUNCIATION
Sound and spelling: *a*

a How is the underlined letter *a* pronounced in each word in the box? Complete the table with the words.

plant   abroad   save   along   dam   danger   nature
park   local   gorilla   mammal   education   after
animal   branch   charity

Sound 1 /eɪ/ (e.g. *paper*)	Sound 2 /ɑː/ (e.g. *glass*)	Sound 3 /æ/ (e.g. *and*)	Sound 4 /ə/ (e.g. *climate*)

b ▶ **5.1** Listen and check.

1 GRAMMAR Zero and first conditional

a Put the words in the correct order to make sentences.

1 going / offer me / to London / I'm / the job, / if / move / they / to .
If they offer me the job, I'm going to move to London.

2 when / at / plane / we'll / Glasgow Airport / phone / lands / our / you .
_____

3 tigers, / if / extinct / we / they'll / stop hunting / don't / 20 years' time / be / in .
_____

4 too / the / when / cold, / south / birds / gets / weather / fly / the .
_____

5 new laptop / my / a / help him / I / the house / dad / buy me / if / paint / will .
_____

6 or an / you / later, / apple / if / feel hungry / have / a banana .
_____

7 11 o'clock / the / be there / with / train / problem / unless / at / a / i'll / there's .
_____

8 take / the / soon, / a / I'm / unless / going to / comes / taxi / bus .
_____

b ▶ 5.2 Listen and check.

c Underline the correct words to complete the sentences.

1 If they *win* / *will win* / *are winning* the match tomorrow, *they're* / *they'll be* / *they were* champions.

2 If you *will see* / *see* / *don't see* Kate tomorrow, *give* / *you'll give* / *you're going to give* her an invitation to the party.

3 When the chameleon *will go* / *goes* / *is going to go* into a different environment, its skin *will change* / *is going to change* / *changes* colour.

4 *Unless* / *If* / *When* it stops raining soon, we *couldn't* / *can't* / *won't be able to* go to the beach this afternoon.

5 *You will open* / *Open* / *You're going to open* the window if you *feel* / *will feel* / *don't feel* too hot.

6 If *she's going to miss* / *she'll miss* / *she misses* the last train this evening, she *had to* / *will have to* / *has to* come tomorrow instead.

7 When the sun *will go* / *goes* / *is going to go* behind the clouds, it *usually feels* / *will usually feel* / *usually felt* much colder.

8 He *can't* / *won't be able to* / *couldn't* find your house unless you *will send* / *are going to send* / *send* him a map.

2 VOCABULARY The natural world

a Look at the animals and label the pictures. Use the words in the box.

petal   scales   paws   tail   branch
web   fur   ~~skin~~   feathers

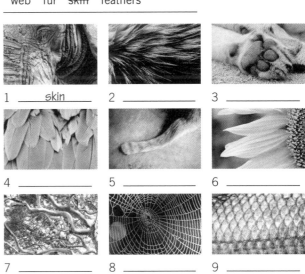

1 ___skin___   2 _____   3 _____

4 _____   5 _____   6 _____

7 _____   8 _____   9 _____

b Complete the crossword puzzle.

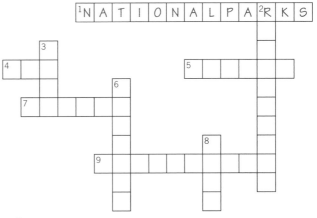

| ¹N | A | T | I | O | N | A | L | P | A | ²R | K | S |

→ **Across**

1 One of the most famous _____ _____ in the USA is Yosemite in California.

4 I'd love to have a house by the _____. It would be lovely to go for a walk on a beach every day.

5 There are five _____ in the world – the Pacific, the Atlantic, the Indian, the Arctic and the Southern Antarctic.

7 The largest _____ in Africa is the Sahara.

9 The highest _____ in the world are the Angel Falls in Venezuela.

↓ **Down**

2 Large areas of the Amazon _____ are destroyed every year.

3 The largest _____ in the world is Superior, on the border between Canada and the USA.

6 _____ are usually much smaller than rivers.

8 In 1940 four French teenagers discovered prehistoric paintings in an underground _____ in Lascaux in the south-west of France.

1 USEFUL LANGUAGE
Reasons, results and examples

a Complete the sentences with the words in the box.

---
like   as a result   due to   because of
for instance   ~~because~~   such as   since   so
---

1 Alice doesn't enjoy her current job ___because___ she often has to work until 8 pm.
2 There are lots of things I can offer this company, _____ my talent for creating attractive websites and my experience of management.
3 It took me over an hour to get to work this morning _____ a serious accident on the motorway.
4 **A** There are some things I don't like about my job.
  B _____?
  A Well, _____, I don't like having to drive 50 km to work every day.
5 Tom didn't get on with his new boss _____ he decided to apply for a job with another company.
6 _____ there weren't any meeting rooms free at 11 o'clock, they had to hold the meeting in his office.
7 I had to stay late at work yesterday. _____, I didn't get home until nine o'clock.
8 My train arrived 45 minutes late this morning _____ the bad weather in Scotland.

b ▶ **5.3** Listen and check.

2 CONVERSATION SKILLS
Giving yourself time to think

a Complete the sentences with the words in the box.

---
second   well   sure   ~~see~~   question
---

1 **A** So how old is your father now?
  B Let me ___see___. I think he'll be 62 in June.
2 **A** So what skills can you bring to this job?
  B _____, to begin with, I've got excellent computer skills.
3 **A** So why do you want to leave your current job?
  B That's a good _____. The main reason is that I need a new challenge.
4 **A** What time does their plane arrive at Heathrow Airport?
  B Just a _____. I'll check on their website.

b ▶ **5.4** Listen and check.

3 PRONUNCIATION
Voiced and unvoiced consonants

a ▶ **5.5** Listen to the pairs of words. Tick (✓) the words you hear.

1 ☐ paw   ✓ bore
2 ☐ pear   ☐ bear
3 ☐ cap   ☐ cab
4 ☐ plume ☐ bloom
5 ☐ cup   ☐ cub

1 READING

a Read the essay and <u>underline</u> the correct phrases to complete the text.

b Read the essay again and tick (✓) the correct answer.

In the writer's opinion …
a ☐ petrol cars are more efficient than electric cars.
b ☐ diesel cars are more environmentally friendly than electric cars.
c ☐ electric cars are better now than a few years ago.
d ☐ people should buy petrol cars in the future.

c Are the sentences true or false?

1 Electric cars are more expensive now than they were a few years ago.
2 Electric cars do not cause problems for the environment.
3 Some people become stressed due to the noise caused by traffic.
4 It costs the same to operate electric cars and petrol cars.
5 You can easily recharge your electric car at home.

Electric cars are the future

If you are thinking of buying a new car soon, perhaps you should consider getting an electric car. In the last few years electric cars have become more efficient and they're now much cheaper to buy. So why should we switch to electric cars?

[1]*In conclusion / First of all / Finally*, air pollution in our cities has become a serious problem over the past 50 years or so. Electric cars do not produce any CO_2 emissions and as a result they don't pollute the atmosphere. If we drive electric cars, this will significantly improve the quality of the air we breathe.

[2]*Firstly / Finally / Secondly*, electric cars are quieter than cars which use petrol or diesel. Today's cars and lorries cause a lot of noise pollution and this can make people feel very stressed.

[3]*Secondly / Finally / First of all*, they are cheaper to operate than conventional cars. The price of petrol is extremely high and the cost per kilometre of an electric car is much lower than a petrol or diesel car. In addition, it is more convenient to recharge your electric car at home than to drive to a petrol station to re-fuel.

[4]*In conclusion / First of all / In addition*, I would say that if we really care about the environment we should all consider buying electric cars. They have improved a great deal in recent years and they will definitely be the vehicle of the future.

2 WRITING

a Read the notes. Write an essay about the advantages of solar panels.

Notes for essay about solar panels

Spend too much on electricity? Solar panels may be the solution.

1) Efficient and good for environment. No pollution, e.g. no carbon dioxide or other gases. If plenty of sunshine, can generate all electricity for the home.

2) Not cheap to buy, but will save money on electricity bills in long term & energy companies buy extra electricity produced. Result: may actually make money.

3) Can increase value of house. People pay higher price to save money on electricity.

4) Conclusion. A good idea. Environmentally friendly & cheap electricity.

UNIT 5
Reading and listening extension

1 READING

a Read the student's essay. Match the paragraphs A–D with functions 1–6. There are two extra functions you do not need.

- [ ] Paragraph A
- [ ] Paragraph B
- [ ] Paragraph C
- [ ] Paragraph D

1 To describe the consequences of climate change
2 To describe weather problems
3 To give the student's own opinion
4 To introduce the main topic and explain the purpose of the essay
5 To show why climate change might be true
6 To show why climate change might not be true

b Read the essay again and tick (✓) the correct answer.

1 According to environmental scientists, …
   - a [ ] forest fires and snow have changed the world's climate.
   - b [ ] pollution has created problems all around the world.
   - c [ ] it is not possible to protect the environment from climate change.

2 The writer explains that the purpose of her essay is …
   - a [ ] to consider two different opinions about climate change.
   - b [ ] to prove that climate change does not really exist.
   - c [ ] to prove that environmental scientists are telling the truth.

3 Why did scientists change their minds in the 1970s?
   - a [ ] because the weather changed unexpectedly
   - b [ ] because they could not predict changes in the weather
   - c [ ] because world temperatures had increased

4 The writer's main purpose in paragraph B is to show …
   - a [ ] how the world's weather changed after World War II.
   - b [ ] that scientists often disagree with each other.
   - c [ ] why some people might not believe in climate change.

5 According to the writer, why is it difficult to predict the weather?
   - a [ ] Environmental scientists do not have the correct equipment.
   - b [ ] The environment never stays the same for very long.
   - c [ ] There are not enough scientists to make accurate predictions.

6 The writer's main purpose in paragraph C is to show …
   - a [ ] how difficult it can be to make accurate predictions.
   - b [ ] why scientists are wrong about climate change.
   - c [ ] why we should believe environmental scientists.

7 According to the writer, …
   - a [ ] it is not possible to protect the environment from pollution.
   - b [ ] terrible weather proves that climate change exists.
   - c [ ] we should not trust the predictions of environmental scientists.

'There is no such thing as climate change. Environmental scientists have been lying to us.' Discuss.

A All around the world, we hear stories of terrible weather becoming even worse. For instance, while forests in Australia are on fire, fields in Egypt are covered in snow. Environmental scientists explain that events such as these are due to climate change. They say that if we cannot protect the environment from pollution, we will definitely destroy the Earth, and everything and everyone that lives on it. Despite this, there are still many people who say that scientists have been lying to us and there is no such thing as climate change. This essay will look at both sides of the argument to see who is telling the truth.

B First of all, it is necessary to remember that scientific opinion has changed many times since the end of the Second World War. For example, in the 1950s, average temperatures in many countries seemed to be rising. Some of the world's best scientists said that this proved that the world was becoming hotter. However, in the early 1970s the world began to freeze. Many countries had the worst winters they had ever known. As a result, scientists made new predictions: the world was not becoming hotter, but much colder. After the freezing winters of the 1970s, world temperatures began to rise again in the 1980s and 1990s. Scientists changed their predictions again and decided that the world was now becoming too hot.

C Some people have said that these examples prove that climate change does not exist. And it is true that scientists have made mistakes. However, I don't believe this means that they are wrong about climate change. Even with advanced technology, it is very difficult to make predictions about the future of weather. The environment is very complex. It consists of billions of creatures and we should also remember that natural environments such as jungles, deserts and mountains are also alive. Therefore it is hard for environmental scientists to make accurate predictions about the weather because all living things change all the time. So although scientific predictions can sometimes be wrong, it does not mean that climate change is not real.

D In conclusion, environmental scientists have not invented climate change. They have made mistakes but the important point is not whether the world is becoming hotter or colder but that the climate is becoming worse. We have an opportunity to prevent climate change and take action.

c Write an essay. Read the question below. Then use the Internet to find ideas, facts and information which agree and disagree with the statement. Decide whether you agree or disagree with the statement in the question.

> 'Climate change is natural – sometimes the earth's temperature is hot, other times it is cold. Climate change is not a consequence of pollution.' Discuss.

2 LISTENING

a ▶ 5.6 Listen to the introduction of a lecture. Then put these parts of the introduction in the correct order.

- ☐ He describes a result of not looking after the environment.
- ☐ He explains how the talk will be organised.
- ☐ He explains why local problems are important.
- ☐ He gives the title of his talk.
- ☐ 1 He uses a story to explain a main idea of the lecture.

b Listen again. Are the sentences true or false?

1 The writer Theodore Dalrymple sees many different kinds of rubbish in the streets.
2 The lecturer says that people need to understand that the environment includes towns and cities.
3 The lecturer says people must save the environment before they make their streets clean and tidy.
4 The lecturer explains that we need to invent more environmentally friendly methods of clearing up rubbish.
5 The talk will include a description of how we can change people's ideas.
6 The lecturer believes that people must make small changes before they can make bigger ones.

c Write a letter to a newspaper about a problem with your local environment. For example:

There's too much rubbish in the local parks.

Remember to include:

- the consequences of not doing anything about the problem
- solutions to the problem
- why some people may disagree with your ideas
- what you say to the people who disagree with your solution.

---

1 GRAMMAR

Correct the sentences.

1 What time will we meet outside the cinema?
  What time shall we meet outside the cinema?
2 If he'll arrive before 2.00, we'll take him to that Italian restaurant for lunch.
3 Wait! I help you do the shopping if you like.
4 Unless it will rain this afternoon, we play golf.
5 I can't come with you because I will play tennis with Joe this afternoon. We meet at the tennis club at 3.00.
6 When they will win the next game, they'll win the gold medal.

2 VOCABULARY

Correct the sentences.

1 We must do everything we can to protect the nature.
  We must do everything we can to protect the environment.
2 There are fantastic beaches on the cost near Rio de Janeiro.
3 It hardly ever rains in the dessert.
4 Air dirt is a serious problem in big cities like Tokyo.
5 The leafs of that tree are as big as my hand.
6 She's working on a very important project to safe endangered species from extinction.

3 WORDPOWER *problem*

Complete the sentences with the words in the box. You might need to change the verb form.

| cause | tackle | be aware of | face | fix | ~~solve~~ |

1 The IT Department ___solved___ the problem with my computer immediately.
2 I'm sure the mechanic will _____ your car.
3 Sometimes it _____ problems on your computer if you install a new program while other programs are open.
4 The government has just launched a new campaign to try to _____ obesity among teenagers.
5 These days most people _____ the problem of deforestation in the Amazon Rainforest.
6 My baseball team are _____ a big problem after losing their last five matches.

♻ REVIEW YOUR PROGRESS

Look again at Review your progress on p.66 of the Student's Book. How well can you do these things now?
3 = very well   2 = well   1 = not so well

I CAN ...

talk about the future	☐
talk about *if* and *when*	☐
give reasons, results and examples	☐
write a discussion essay.	☐

6A You have to use pedestrian crossings

1 GRAMMAR Modals of obligation

a Underline the correct words to complete the conversation.

PAUL I've got my English exam tomorrow morning.

MUM Oh, really? So what time do you [1]*should / have to / must* be at school?

PAUL Well, the exam starts at 9 o'clock, so I [2]*mustn't / don't have to / can* be late.

MUM I think you [3]*shouldn't / mustn't / ought to* leave earlier than normal, in case there's a lot of traffic.

PAUL Yes, that's a good idea.

MUM And what are you going to do after the exam?

PAUL Well, I [4]*mustn't / shouldn't / don't have to* stay at school in the afternoon, so I [5]*can / should / must* come home for lunch.

MUM Fine, just two more things. It says on this information sheet that students [6]*can / must / shouldn't* show their identity cards to the examiner before the exam.

PAUL Don't worry. I always take my ID card with me to school.

MUM It also says you [7]*don't have to / must / can't* use a dictionary during the exam, so don't take one with you.

PAUL Yes, I know. I'll leave it at home.

MUM OK, good. By the way, it's 10 o'clock. You [8]*shouldn't / have to / must* go to bed late tonight.

PAUL No, you're right. I'll go up now.

MUM OK, good night. And good luck for tomorrow!

b ▶ 6.1 Listen and check.

c Match 1–6 with a–f to make sentences.

1 f The service was terrible, so you shouldn't
2 ☐ Go slower! We're near a school so you mustn't
3 ☐ In my experience you don't usually have to
4 ☐ I'm worried about hiring a car in the USA. I think we should
5 ☐ It's all right here. The sign says you can
6 ☐ It's Mum's birthday tomorrow. You've got to

a take off your shoes when you go into a British person's house.
b drive more than 50 kilometres per hour.
c buy her a present this afternoon.
d park your car here after 6.30 pm.
e read about the rules for driving in the guidebook before we decide.
f give the waiter a tip.

2 VOCABULARY Compound nouns

a Match 1–6 with a–f to make sentences.

1 c When I go into the town centre I normally use public
2 ☐ I haven't got any money on me, so I'll go to the cash
3 ☐ The car didn't stop when the traffic
4 ☐ I think they should put a pedestrian
5 ☐ It's safe to cycle to work because there are cycle
6 ☐ I hate driving into London in the rush

a lanes so you're not on the road with all the cars.
b crossing outside the school, as it's a dangerous road to cross.
c transport, as the car parks are very expensive.
d machine outside the bank opposite the station.
e hour, so I leave home at 6.30 most days.
f lights turned red and crashed into a bus.

3 VOCABULARY Multi-word verbs

a Underline the correct words to complete the sentences.

1 The easiest way to get *out / around / away* London is to take the underground.
2 Restaurants are quite expensive in Paris so my wife and I only eat *around / away / out* once or twice a month.
3 If Sarah doesn't turn *away / out / up* soon, I think we should buy our tickets for the film and go in without her.
4 I've got a cousin that lives in New York, so I'm sure he'll be able to show us *around / up / out* the city.
5 Although I lived in Stockholm for a year, I didn't pick *out / up / back* much Swedish because everyone speaks English.
6 We've got three hours before we need to go, so why don't we look *back / around / up* the town for a couple of hours?
7 I'm tired after all this sightseeing, so I'd like to go *out / up / back* to the hotel now, if that's OK with you.
8 We normally go *away / out / back* for two or three weeks every summer but we can't afford a holiday this year.

4 PRONUNCIATION Word stress

a ▶ 6.2 Listen to the compound nouns and underline the stressed syllables.

1 swimming pool   4 cycle lane
2 rush hour   5 lunchtime
3 washing machine   6 cash machine

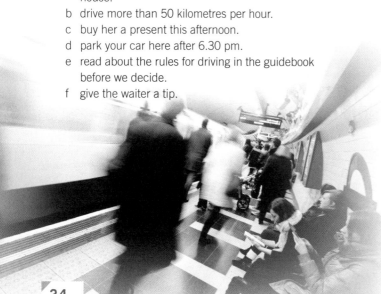

6B It's tastier than I expected

1 GRAMMAR
Comparatives and superlatives

a Put the words in the correct order to make sentences.

1 wasn't / as / my / nearly / I / nice / as / meal / expected .
   My meal wasn't nearly as nice as I expected.

2 by far / is / luxurious / the / most / I've / hotel / stayed in / this / ever .
   _____

3 than / tennis / much / I do / plays / she / better .
   _____

4 nearly / today / hot / as / was / as / isn't / yesterday / it .
   _____

5 most / these / are / ever / shoes / expensive / I've / the / bought .
   _____

6 cheaper / go to / the restaurant / we / far / normally / this restaurant / is / than .
   _____

7 hardest / that was / the / I've / my / in / exam / taken / life .
   _____

8 got / yesterday / than / usual / earlier / home / she / evening .
   _____

b ▶ **6.3** Listen and check.

c Correct two mistakes in each sentence.

1 He speaks quicklier that I do.
   He speaks more quickly than I do.

2 London is many expensiver than Edinburgh.
   _____

3 They make the better pizzas of Rome.
   _____

4 Colin is more clever that his brother.
   _____

5 That was the most sad film I ever seen.
   _____

6 The exam wasn't near as hard that I expected.
   _____

7 I think this is most simple recipe in the book.
   _____

8 At the moment the weather in France is a little more warm that in the UK.
   _____

d ▶ **6.4** Listen and check.

2 VOCABULARY Describing food

a Underline the correct words to complete the sentences.

1 This coffee is too *sour* / *bitter* / <u>*sweet*</u>. You know I don't take sugar!

2 To make a Spanish omelette add the *creamy* / *heavy* / *cooked* onions and potatoes to the eggs and then fry the mixture for about five minutes.

3 When you make a salad, it's better to use *cooked* / *raw* / *sour* carrots so they don't lose their vitamins.

4 Sorry, I can't eat these cornflakes quietly. They're really *crunchy* / *sour* / *raw*.

5 It's the butter and the milk in this sauce that makes it taste so *crunchy* / *creamy* / *sour*.

6 This cream's horrible. It tastes really *dried* / *heavy* / *sour*. When did you buy it?

7 It's always better to use *fresh* / *sweet* / *heavy* herbs when you're cooking. They taste much nicer.

8 I had a really *light* / *raw* / *heavy* dinner last night so I didn't sleep very well.

b Complete the sentences with the words in the box.

add	stir	mix	mash	chop
fry	~~squeeze~~	serve	heat up	

1 You need to ___squeeze___ the juice from four large oranges to make a glass of orange juice.

2 When the potatoes are cooked, take them out of the water and then _____ them with a little butter and milk until they are smooth and creamy.

3 Using a sharp knife, _____ the onions and peppers finely and then _____ them in a little olive oil for about five minutes.

4 _____ a little salt and pepper to the tomato sauce and cook it slowly for about twenty minutes.

5 To make the salad, _____ the lettuce, tomatoes, onions and cucumber together, put a little olive oil and balsamic vinegar on top and _____ with some fresh bread and butter.

6 _____ the mixture of milk, butter and flour in a saucepan and _____ continuously with a wooden spoon to ensure a smooth, creamy sauce.

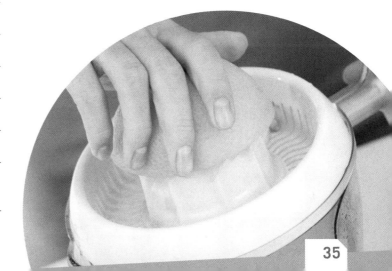

6C Everyday English

Do you think I should take her somewhere special?

1 USEFUL LANGUAGE Asking for and giving recommendations

a Complete the conversation with the words in the box.

| worth | should | ~~think~~ | idea | kidding | were |
| better | recommend | would | definitely |

A So, where do you ¹___think___ I should take my mother on holiday?

B If I ²_____ you, I'd take her somewhere warm, like Italy.

A You've been to Italy lots of times, haven't you? Where would you ³_____ taking her?

B Well, you should ⁴_____ go to Rome – it's such a beautiful city.

A That's a good idea. And when ⁵_____ you go?

B Er, let me see. Well, it's not a good ⁶_____ to go in July or August, as it's much too hot for sightseeing then. It's much ⁷_____ to go in May or June, when it isn't quite as hot.

A And where do you think we ⁸_____ stay in Rome?

B Well, there are some lovely hotels in the centre, but they're at least €200 a night.

A You're ⁹_____! I had no idea it would be that expensive. I can't afford to pay that much!

B Oh, well, in that case it's probably ¹⁰_____ finding a hotel outside the centre, then.

A Yes, that makes sense. Thanks for your advice.

b ▶ **6.5** Listen and check.

c Underline the correct words to complete the sentences.

1. You should definitely *to visit* / *visiting* / *visit* the British Museum when you're in London.
2. What dress would you *wearing* / *wear* / *to wear* to the party?
3. It's much better *take* / *to take* / *taking* the train from London to Paris.
4. Would you recommend *going* / *to go* / *go* to Athens in August?
5. It's probably worth *book* / *booking* / *to book* a hotel before you go.
6. If I were you, *I'll* / *I did* / *I'd* take the job in San Francisco.
7. Do you think I *would* / *should* / *shall* buy this watch?
8. It's not a good idea *to change* / *changing* / *change* your money at the airport.

d ▶ **6.6** Listen and check.

2 PRONUNCIATION Sounding interested

a ▶ **6.7** Listen to the exchanges. Does Speaker B sound excited or bored? Tick (✓) the correct box.

1. **A** My boyfriend's taking me to Paris this weekend!
   B Wow! That's amazing.   excited ✓ bored ☐

2. **A** I've been offered a place at Harvard University!
   B Oh, really? That's good.   excited ☐ bored ☐

3. **A** I got the best exam grades in my class!
   B That's amazing! Well done!   excited ☐ bored ☐

4. **A** My dad's going to buy me a rabbit!
   B Wow! That's brilliant.   excited ☐ bored ☐

5. **A** John's asked me to marry him!
   B Great! I'm so happy for you. excited ☐ bored ☐

6. **A** We're going on holiday on Saturday!
   B I know. I can't wait!   excited ☐ bored ☐

Skills for Writing
It's definitely worth a visit

'The tastiest Italian food in London?'   `Review A`

I took my Italian friend here for his birthday and he absolutely loved it. The atmosphere was really relaxing and the waiters were friendly and extremely helpful. All the food was really fresh and the portions were generous. The tiramisu that we had for our dessert was absolutely delicious. Paolo says it's the best he's ever had – apart from his mum's, of course! Although our meal was rather expensive, we didn't mind paying a bit more than usual because the food was so good. I'd definitely recommend this restaurant if you want to eat lovely food in a relaxing atmosphere.   **EMMA T**

'Not the most relaxing evening …'   `Review B`

A colleague at work recommended this place but we thought it was rather disappointing. First of all, the atmosphere wasn't very relaxing. It was a bit noisy, perhaps because it was a Friday night and the restaurant was rather busy. Also, the music was too loud so it was hard to talk. Secondly, although the waiters were very friendly, there weren't enough of them when we were there and so the service was slow. Unfortunately, when our food eventually arrived it wasn't very good. Our steaks were a bit overcooked and the salad wasn't very fresh. Finally, the portions weren't very big and we thought the meal was rather overpriced. All in all, I'm afraid I wouldn't recommend it.   **DAVID M**

1 READING

a Read the reviews and tick (✓) the correct column.

	Review A	Review B
1 The reviewer really enjoyed the meal.		
2 The service wasn't very good.		
3 The quality of the food was good.		
4 The review of the restaurant is positive.		

b Read the reviews again. Are the sentences true or false?

1 In Emma's opinion, the service was good.
2 Emma didn't enjoy her dessert.
3 Emma thought the price of her meal was too high.
4 There weren't many people there when David went to this restaurant.
5 David had to wait a long time for his food to arrive.
6 David was rather disappointed by the quality of his food.

2 WRITING SKILLS Positive and negative language; Adverbs

a <u>Underline</u> the correct words to complete the sentences with a 'strong' or a 'weak' adverb, following the instruction in brackets.

1 The chocolate cake was *fairly* / <u>*absolutely*</u> delicious. (strong)
2 Unfortunately, all the vegetables were *rather* / *completely* overcooked. (weak)
3 The food in that new restaurant was *extremely* / *a bit* boring. (weak)
4 I thought the portions were *absolutely tiny* / *rather small*. (weak)
5 That new café is *extremely* / *fairly* expensive. (strong)
6 I thought the tomato soup was *rather* / *completely* tasteless. (strong)
7 The staff in the hotel were *reasonably* / *really* friendly. (weak)
8 When we were there the service was *quite* / *terribly* slow. (strong)

3 WRITING

a Write two reviews, one for each of the restaurants in the fact files below. One review should be mostly positive, the other mostly negative.

RESTAURANT FACT FILE

NAME:	Chez Pierre
LOCATION:	city centre
TYPE OF FOOD:	French e.g. meat (steak, lamb, etc.), fish / seafood, salads
QUALITY OF FOOD:	
ATMOSPHERE:	
MUSIC:	
TYPE OF CUSTOMER:	businessmen and women, romantic couples
SERVICE/ATTITUDE OF WAITERS:	
PRICE:	££££
VALUE FOR MONEY:	
WHEN BUSY:	Weekday lunchtimes, weekends

RESTAURANT FACT FILE

NAME:	Villa Borghese
LOCATION:	at the beach
TYPE OF FOOD:	Italian e.g. pizzas, pasta risotto, fish, meat, ice cream
QUALITY OF FOOD:	
ATMOSPHERE:	
MUSIC:	
TYPE OF CUSTOMER:	families and groups of young people
SERVICE/ATTITUDE OF WAITERS:	
PRICE:	£
VALUE FOR MONEY:	
WHEN BUSY:	every evening

UNIT 6
Reading and listening extension

1 READING

a Read the text. Are the sentences true or false?

1 This text is a newspaper article.
2 The writer's name is Alex Walker.
3 The writer says that she enjoyed her first visit to the city despite one or two problems.
4 The writer says that the city has improved.

b Read the text again and tick (✓) the correct answers.

1 How long has Alex Walker been mayor of the city?
a ☐ at least one year
b ☐ exactly one year
c ☐ less than one year

2 What does Ayesha say about taxis during her first visit?
a ☐ It was impossible for her to find one.
b ☐ She was not able to use them.
c ☐ They were better than public transport.

3 Why is Ayesha writing another report about the city?
a ☐ She had been invited to an anniversary party in the city.
b ☐ She has become a professional journalist.
c ☐ She heard that a lot of money had been spent on the city.

4 How has the train station improved since Ayesha's last visit?
a ☐ Men are employed to help her get from the platform to the exit.
b ☐ She can get from the platform to the exit by herself.
c ☐ They have repaired the old lifts on the platform.

5 How many of the cash machines at the station can Ayesha use easily?
a ☐ one
b ☐ two
c ☐ three

6 How many different forms of transport did Ayesha use to get around the city?
a ☐ one
b ☐ two
c ☐ three

c Think about the place where you live. How easy or difficult do you think it might be for wheelchair users to get around your hometown? Make notes about:

- public transport (do buses/trains/trams have disabled access?)
- things to do and places to visit (is it easy to visit a museum or go shopping?)

Use your notes to write a short review of disabled access for wheelchair users where you live.

CITY MAKES PROGRESS FOR DISABLED

This week is the first anniversary of mayor Alex Walker's promise to make life in our city easier for disabled people. One year on, we asked disabled athlete Ayesha Omar to tell us about her experiences in the city.

Just over a year ago, City News invited me here for the day to do an interview; it turned out to be a visit I will never forget – unfortunately, for all the wrong reasons. As someone in a wheelchair, it was almost impossible for me to get around the city. There was not nearly enough access to public transport and I discovered that taxis were no better: none of them had the special doors I need to carry my wheelchair. The day was such a nightmare that I decided to write a story about my experience in the paper. After I wrote my story, mayor Alex Walker promised to make things better in the city and gave £6 million to the project. Last week, I returned to see if the city had improved.

I arrived at the train station early in the morning. One year ago, the station had only had stairs up to the exit. That meant that three men had to carry me off the platform which was by far the most embarrassing thing that happened to me during my last visit. This year, I saw immediately that they had built a new lift. 'Wonderful!' I thought – but then I remembered something – the buttons. On 'normal' lifts, the buttons are sometimes too high for a person in a wheelchair. That means that I have to ask someone to push the buttons for me. However, the lift in the station had buttons that were much lower so I was able to push them myself. I was really pleased with this.

I decided to take a taxi into the city centre, so first of all I needed to get some money from the bank. Again, I am very pleased to say that when I found the line of three cash machines outside the station, one of them was lower than the other two and so it was the right height for wheelchair users. Later that day, I took a bus and a tram and visited all the main museums, galleries and shopping centres. There was access for wheelchair users everywhere I went. Things are still not perfect and there is a long way to go but I can honestly say that Alex Walker has kept his promise to disabled people in the city!

2 LISTENING

a ▶ **6.8** Listen to a conversation between three students, Peeraya, Sylvie and Matt, and tick (✓) the correct answers.

1 Which two students are meeting for the first time?
  - a ☐ Peeraya and Matt
  - b ☐ Peeraya and Sylvie
  - c ☐ Sylvie and Matt

2 How do Peeraya and Sylvie know each other?
  - a ☐ They are going to Liverpool together.
  - b ☐ They study English together.
  - c ☐ They met on holiday in Thailand.

3 Peeraya and Sylvie ask Matt to …
  - a ☐ recommend a good, local restaurant.
  - b ☐ explain how to make fish and chips.
  - c ☐ tell them the best place to get a burger.

4 At the end of the conversation, Peeraya and Sylvie …
  - a ☐ agree with Matt's recommendation.
  - b ☐ ask Matt to recommend something else.
  - c ☐ decide to ask someone else.

b Listen again. <u>Underline</u> the correct words to complete the sentences.

1 Peeraya and Sylvie are planning a celebration for *the end of their English course* / *their friend's birthday* / *passing their English exams*.

2 Matt says that he has lived in Liverpool *for quite a long time* / *for quite a short time* / *all his life*.

3 Peeraya and Sylvie will be inviting *18* / *20* / *21* people to the celebration.

4 Sylvie does not want to go to a *big* / *chain* / *family* restaurant.

5 Both Peeraya and Sylvie would like to try *British fish and chips* / *hot and spicy Thai seafood* / *traditional English dishes*.

6 'Scouse' is a traditional *dessert* / *meat dish* / *vegetarian dish* from Liverpool.

7 To get to 'Sarah's Bistro' Peeraya and Sylvie should *turn right* / *turn left* / *go straight on* at the cash machine on Double Street.

c Write a conversation between two people discussing how to celebrate the end of their English course. Use the questions below to help you.
  - How many people will go?
  - Where will they go to eat? Will the place be big enough?
  - Is anyone in the class a vegetarian?
  - Is there any type of food that someone in the class cannot eat (for example, fish)?

Review and extension

1 GRAMMAR

Correct the sentences.

1 You must to arrive 30 minutes before the exam starts.
  You must arrive 30 minutes before the exam starts.
2 I think this is the better Greek restaurant in London.
3 Last night we must take a taxi because we'd missed the bus.
4 His house is more near the university than yours.
5 You mustn't parking outside that school.
6 He's more taller than his older brother.
7 You don't have to feed the animals in the zoo – it's forbidden.
8 I think French is easyer to learn than English.

2 VOCABULARY

Correct the sentences and questions.

1 When he realised he'd forgotten his passport, he came back to his house to get it.
  When he realised he'd forgotten his passport, he went back to his house to get it.
2 Can I borrow your spoon so I can mix my coffee?
3 We had three hours to wait so we saw round the old town.
4 The best way to move around New York is to take the subway.
5 Mash the lemon and pour the juice over the fish.
6 If you put in too much sugar, it will be too sour to drink.

3 WORDPOWER *go*

Match 1–6 with a–f to make sentences.

1 ☐d I don't think anything can go
2 ☐ My English exam went
3 ☐ Unfortunately, all the tickets had gone
4 ☐ The stairs next to the lift go
5 ☐ The tie you bought yesterday goes
6 ☐ My father's hair has all gone

a really well with your blue shirt.
b down to the car park.
c by the time we got there.
d wrong because it's a brilliant plan.
e grey now but it was fair when he was young.
f really well. I think I passed.

REVIEW YOUR PROGRESS

Look again at Review your progress on p.78 of the Student's Book. How well can you do these things now?
3 = very well   2 = well   1 = not so well

I CAN …

talk about advice and rules	☐
describe food	☐
ask for and give recommendations	☐
write a review of a restaurant or café.	☐

1 GRAMMAR Modals of deduction

a Match 1–8 with a–h to make pairs of sentences.

1 [g] They may have some relatives in Miami.
2 [ ] She can't live in that tiny flat.
3 [ ] Their car's outside the house, but I haven't seen them for a few days.
4 [ ] There are a lot of people in our neighbour's garden.
5 [ ] Why's Sam wearing a suit and tie?
6 [ ] She can't still be living with her parents.
7 [ ] He might not have a well-paid job at the moment.

a They could be away on holiday.
b That's why he isn't taking his family on holiday this year.
c They might be having a party.
d She's nearly 40 years old.
e She told me she had four bedrooms and two bathrooms.
f He must be going to London today for his job interview.
g Perhaps that's why they always go there every January?

b Underline the correct words to complete the conversation.

A Some new people have just moved into the house opposite.
B Yes, I know. I saw them yesterday when they arrived. I think they're French.
A No, they [1]*mustn't / can't / must* be French. Their car has a 'P' sticker on the back.
B Oh, really? They [2]*can't / couldn't / might* come from Poland, then.
A Or they [3]*mustn't / could / can't* be Portuguese?
B That's true – both countries begin with a 'P'.
A Is it a family or a couple?
B It [4]*must / can't / couldn't* be a family. They [5]*couldn't / must / mustn't* have two or three children.
A How do you know that?
B Because I saw some children's bikes in their garden. Also, there was another woman in the car when they arrived yesterday – she was older than the mother.
A She [6]*might / can / couldn't* be the children's grandmother.
B No, she [7]*can / mustn't / can't* be their grandmother. She only looked about 45.
A Or she [8]*must / can't / could* be their aunt? Or she [9]*can't / might not / can* be a relative at all. She [10]*may / can't / can* be just a friend. She [11]*can't / might / can* be helping them to unpack their things.
B Why don't we go and say 'hello'?
A But they [12]*might not / can't / couldn't* speak English – it [13]*can't / could / mustn't* be really embarrassing.
B They [14]*can't / couldn't / must* speak English. I just saw them speaking to one of their neighbours and they seemed to understand each other.

c ▶ 7.1 Listen and check.

2 VOCABULARY Buildings

a Complete the crossword puzzle.

→ **Across**
2 I used to live in a very noisy ____block____ of flats.
6 I'd like to live in a friendly _____ that has a good primary school for my children.
7 I had a good _____ of the sea from my hotel window.
8 My office is on the 22nd _____ so I take the lift.

↓ **Down**
1 His new house is in a very convenient _____. He can walk to the city centre in five minutes.
3 We had a lovely hotel room with a large _____ outside, where I could read my book and sunbathe.
4 A lot of American houses have a large _____ under the house where the children can watch TV and play.
5 When you get to my building, ring the _____ and I'll come down to meet you.

b Underline the correct words to complete the sentences.

1 At the top of my house there's *a balcony / an attic / a basement* where we keep all the things we don't use any more.
2 When I lived in Rome I *located / hired / rented* a tiny *house / flat / landing* which only had two rooms.
3 Go up the stairs to the *landing / hall / basement* on the first *level / step / floor*. My bedroom is the first on the right.
4 The *principal / front / in front of* door has two *locks / views / steps* so take both keys when you leave the house.
5 I'm moving *off / out of / away* this flat next Saturday and moving *in / on / into* my new flat on Sunday.
6 On the *ground / earth / land* floor there's a huge *pavement / terrace / balcony* where you can sit and relax.

3 PRONUNCIATION
Final sounds in modal verbs

a ▶ 7.2 Listen. Tick (✓) the sentences where you hear the final /t/ or /d/ of the modal verbs.

1 [✓] He mus**t** have rich parents.
2 [ ] She can'**t** be revising for her exams tonight.
3 [ ] They migh**t** enjoy going to the zoo.
4 [ ] You coul**d** invite Jenny to your party.
5 [ ] We mus**t** be quite near the centre now.
6 [ ] John mus**t** earn a lot more money than her.

B There are plenty of things to do

1 GRAMMAR Quantifiers

a Complete the sentences with the words in the box.

> too many   plenty   ~~many~~   no
> some   a few   little   enough (x2)

1 She doesn't have ____many____ clothes so she needs to buy _____.
2 There isn't _____ time to have a meal before the film.
3 There are _____ cars on the roads these days.
4 We've got _____ of time before the film starts, so let's go for a coffee.
5 He knows quite _____ people in London, so he won't be lonely.
6 I'm sorry but there are _____ tickets left for tonight's show.
7 She isn't fit _____ yet to run a marathon.
8 I have very _____ money left so I'm not going out tonight.

b Correct the sentences.

1 I'm late because there was much traffic in the city centre.
   I'm late because there was a lot of traffic in the city
   centre.
2 Unfortunately, there aren't no good restaurants near here.
   _____
3 He won't pass his exams because he hasn't worked enough hard this year.
   _____
4 **A** Is there many milk left?
   _____
   B Yes, we've got plenty of.
   _____
5 There were too much people at the bus stop to get on the bus.
   _____
6 There are too little eggs in the fridge to make a Spanish omelette.
   _____
7 My father's too much old to play tennis these days.
   _____
8 She made lot of mistakes in her translation.
   _____

2 VOCABULARY Verbs and prepositions

a Underline the correct words to complete the sentences.

1 He paid *about* / *around* / _for_ the shopping with his credit card.
2 I complained to the receptionist *about* / *for* / *from* the dirty towels in my room.
3 They apologised to their teacher *about* / *for* / *with* not doing all their homework.
4 We try to recycle all of our rubbish because we care *for* / *about* / *with* the environment.
5 If you get into trouble, you can always depend *about* / *for* / *on* your family to help you.
6 She's thinking *about* / *in* / *at* her boyfriend.
7 It was very hard for the children to cope *about* / *with* / *for* their parents' divorce.
8 After five years in Tokyo he succeeded *for* / *on* / *in* learning Japanese.

b Complete the sentences with one word from each of the boxes.

> rely   complained   ~~believe~~   apologised
> belongs   argued   cope   worried

> to (x2)   with (x2)   about (x2)   ~~in~~   on

1 When I was little I used to ___believe___ ___in___ ghosts.
2 She's finding it hard to _____ _____ the stress of her new job.
3 I _____ _____ Jane for forgetting her birthday.
4 You can always _____ _____ the metro as the trains run very regularly.
5 Dan's getting _____ _____ his job because his company wants to save money.
6 I think that cat _____ _____ one of my neighbours.
7 He went over the road and _____ _____ the noise his neighbour was making.
8 At the end of the meal they _____ _____ the waiter about the bill.

7C Everyday English
Is there anything we can do to help?

1 USEFUL LANGUAGE Offers, requests and asking for permission

a Match the questions 1–6 with the responses a–f.

1. [d] Do you think you could help me with the shopping bags?
2. [ ] Is there anything I can do to help?
3. [ ] Do you think I could have a quick shower?
4. [ ] May I use your phone?
5. [ ] Is it OK if I watch the news on TV?
6. [ ] Would you mind taking your shoes off?

a Sure, no problem. Let me turn it on for you.
b No, not at all. Where shall I leave them?
c Yes, of course. It's in the hall.
d Sure, I'll take them into the kitchen for you.
e Yes, of course. Let me get you a towel.
f Yes, there is, actually. Could you lay the table for me?

b ▶ **7.3** Listen and check.

c Complete the responses with the words in the box. There is one extra word you do not need.

~~course~~ lovely mind sure better control really

1. **A** Do you think I could borrow your camera tomorrow?
   B Yes, of __course__. It's in the living room. Here.
2. **A** I'm sorry about the problem with your computer. Is there anything I can do to help?
   B No, it's fine, _____. I think I can fix it.
3. **A** Do you think you could give me a hand with this maths homework?
   B _____. Let me have a look at it.
4. **A** Are you OK in the kitchen? Let me help you.
   B Don't worry! It's all under _____.
5. **A** Is there anything I can do for the party? I could organise some games for the kids.
   B That would be _____, thanks.
6. **A** Is it OK if I have a cheese sandwich?
   B We can do _____ than that. Come in the kitchen and I'll make you something special for lunch.

d Underline the correct words to complete the sentences.

1. Would you mind *open* / *opening* / *to open* that door for me?
2. Is it OK if I *leave* / *left* / *could leave* my coat here?
3. **A** Do you think *I'd* / *I would* / *I could* have a cup of tea?
   B Yes, of course. *I shall* / *I'll* / *I would* make one for you.
4. **A** Would you mind if *I used* / *I use* / *I'll use* your toilet?
   B Not at all. *Leave* / *Let* / *Allow* me show you where it is.
5. Is there *anything* / *nothing* / *a thing* I can do to help?
6. Excuse me. Do you think you *will* / *could* / *would* turn the music down a little, please? It's really hard to talk in here.

e ▶ **7.4** Listen and check.

2 PRONUNCIATION Sounding polite

a ▶ **7.5** Listen to the pairs of questions. Tick (✓) the question which sounds more polite: a or b.

1. a Would you mind getting me some more water? [✓]
   b Would you mind getting me some more water? [ ]
2. a Do you think you could lend me some money? [ ]
   b Do you think you could lend me some money? [ ]
3. a Is it OK if I make myself a coffee? [ ]
   b Is it OK if I make myself a coffee? [ ]
4. a Do you think I could borrow your car? [ ]
   b Do you think I could borrow your car? [ ]
5. a Do you mind if I make a quick phone call? [ ]
   b Do you mind if I make a quick phone call? [ ]

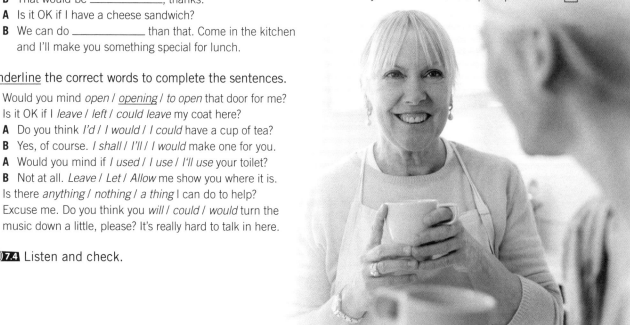

1 READING

a Read the note and tick (✓) the correct answer.

a ☐ Sarah hasn't left any food in her fridge for Paul.
b ☐ You can't walk to the city centre from Sarah's house.
c ☐ Paul's children won't get bored in York.
d ☐ You can go swimming in Rowntree Park.

b Read the note again. Are the sentences true or false?

1 Paul needs to go to the supermarket to buy some bread for breakfast.
2 There aren't any big supermarkets in York.
3 It's easy to take the bus from Sarah's house to the city centre.
4 Paul's children would enjoy a visit to the railway museum.
5 Paul can't go swimming with his children in York.

aul!

:ome to York! Hope you had a good journey from London and
: it wasn't difficult to find my house and get the keys from my
-door neighbour.

 yourself to anything you find in the fridge and the kitchen
oards. For breakfast tomorrow morning you can have cereal
 milk. Otherwise, there's plenty of bread to make toast and
II find butter and strawberry jam in the fridge.

u need to go shopping for lunch or dinner, the nearest
rmarket is the little SPAR in Clifton, the main road from the
centre. You probably passed it on your way to my house.
rnatively, you can drive to the big Tesco on the A1237 at
on Moor, which has everything you need.

he way, you can take the number 2 bus to the centre from the
of my road. The buses run every five minutes or so. Another
on is to walk. It takes about 25 minutes to walk to the centre
 here but it's good exercise.

e are plenty of things to do and see in York. You can take the
 to the Jorvik Viking Centre where they can learn all about the
gs. Another possibility is to visit the National Railway Museum
 the station. I think they'll enjoy going to both places. Apart
 that, there are lots of good shops in the city centre and also
ty of nice cafés and restaurants if you prefer to eat out.

lly, if you need some exercise there's an excellent swimming pool
axby Road. Alternatively, if the weather's nice you and the kids
play tennis in Rowntree Park in Terry Avenue.

way, enjoy your stay and speak soon.

e,

ah

2 WRITING SKILLS Offering choices

a Use one of the words or phrases in the box to connect the sentences. Make any necessary changes. There is more than one possible answer.

Another option is   Otherwise   Alternatively
Apart from that   Another possibility is

1 You can take the train from here to Granada. Or there is a coach which runs every two hours.
<u>You can take the train from here to Granada. Apart from that, there is a coach which runs every two hours.</u>

2 There's a good shop at the end of my road. You could also go to the huge supermarket which is just before you get to the motorway.
_____

3 You can get a good view of London from the London Eye. Or you can go to the top of The Shard building.
_____

4 I suggest you go to the beach early in the morning, before it gets too hot. You could also go late in the afternoon.
_____

5 Why don't you go to that Italian restaurant opposite Covent Garden Underground Station? Or you could try that new Japanese restaurant near Leicester Square.
_____

3 WRITING

a Read the notes. Write a note for Pascale, the babysitter who is going to look after your two young children this evening.

Note for Pascale

1) Drinks & snacks
   · Tea & coffee by kettle. Hot chocolate in cupboard.
   · Chocolate biscuits on table. Cheesecake in fridge.

2) Dinner for children
   · Chicken soup & fish pie in fridge. Sandwiches.

3) Entertainment
   · OK to watch TV (both like X Factor).
   · Favourite DVDs are Toy Story & Pirates of the Caribbean.

4) Bedtime
   · Read bedtime story e.g. Harry Potter / The Lion, the Witch and the Wardrobe.

5) If any problems, phone:
   · 07700 900221 (Me)
   · 07700 900834 (Other person's mobile. Whose?)

UNIT 7
Reading and listening extension

1 READING

a Read the article. Match the paragraphs A–D with functions 1–6. There are two extra functions you do not need.

- [ ] Paragraph A
- [ ] Paragraph B
- [ ] Paragraph C
- [ ] Paragraph D

1　To describe how Detroit changed
2　To explain that education in Detroit has become worse
3　To make a prediction about the future of Detroit
4　To show that Detroit helped a singer become famous
5　To show that Detroit might be improving
6　To show the reader why Detroit is an important place

b Read the text again and put the information in the correct order of the article.

- [ ] a possible benefit of recent changes to Detroit
- [ ] businessmen whose relatives are from Detroit
- [ ] how old parts of Detroit have changed recently
- [ ] other names for Detroit
- [ ] popular songs that came from Detroit
- [1] a businessman who made Detroit famous
- [ ] the number of people who live in Detroit
- [ ] a famous singer who made records in Detroit
- [ ] the way people might think about Detroit in the future
- [ ] where many people in the city used to work

c Think about your hometown or another place that you know well. Make notes about:

- where it is
- how old it is
- some famous people who have lived there
- some things it is famous for / things that you can only find in that place
- some important changes that have happened there in the last 50 years.

Write a short essay about this place.

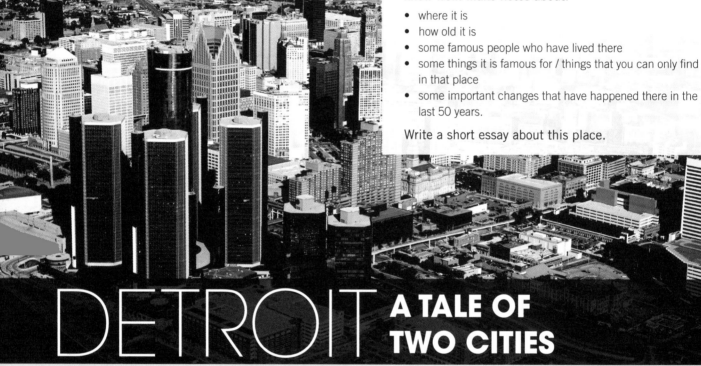

DETROIT A TALE OF TWO CITIES

A　**DETROIT** was at one time one of the most famous cities in the United States, and perhaps even the world. This was the city where Henry Ford built the Ford Motor Company in 1903, and it didn't take long for Detroit to become known as 'Motor City'. Later, 'Motor City' became simply 'Motown', which was, of course, the name given to the popular American music of the 1960s and '70s that came out of the city, including The Jackson 5 – the band where Michael Jackson sang such hits as 'I Want You Back' and 'ABC'. Today, however, Detroit is a very different place.

B　In 1950, the city had a population of 1.8 million and there were nearly 300,000 men and women working in its car factories. Nowadays, that population is just 700,000 and only 27,000 have jobs connected with the car industry. So many people moved out of Detroit after 2001 that by 2010, more than a third of Detroit's houses, factories and schools were empty. In lots of neighbourhoods, not only was there no more noise from the traffic but there was also no more music. The city was so cold and dark that many people thought the city had died. Then businessmen John Hantz and Michael Score moved in.

C　Hantz and Score, who both have family connections in Detroit, cared about what was happening there. They also both believed in the same very simple idea – urban farms. Together, they bought lots of empty land in the city and then pulled down 50 old houses. Instead of broken buildings, there are now fields of trees. Once Hantz and Score had succeeded in showing what could be done with all that empty land, lots of other people started to create their own gardens. Men and women who used to build cars and lorries are now planting fruit and vegetables. And now something even better has happened.

D　In the first ten years of the 21st century, crime increased and many residents became worried about safety on the streets at night. But now, incredibly, crime has fallen and many residents believe this must be due to the new urban farms and gardens. Although it has not been proven whether the new green spaces are the reason that crime has gone down, you can be sure that no one in the city is complaining about it! Perhaps this could be a change other cities around the world could learn from, and it might not be long before 'Motor City' becomes known as 'Green City'.

2 LISTENING

a ▶ **7.6** Listen to a group of friends talking. Match 1–6 with a–f to make sentences.

1 [b] They must
2 [ ] They can't
3 [ ] One of them has to
4 [ ] Some of them have to
5 [ ] Katia is the person who is
6 [ ] Ben is the person who is

a describe a place to the others.
b be playing some kind of game.
c talking about a house.
d explaining how to play the game.
e draw something.
f be in the university library.

b Listen to the conversation again. Tick (✓) the correct answer.

1 On her turn, Katia gets …
  a [ ] three. b [ ] twelve. c [ ] sixteen.

2 Luis and Daniela have to draw what she describes …
  a [ ] on the same piece of paper.
  b [ ] using a special kind of pencil.
  c [ ] without looking at their picture.

3 Where would Katia's dream home be?
  a [ ] in a village
  b [ ] in a small town
  c [ ] in a big city

4 What would Katia be able to see from her dream home?
  a [ ] a beautiful mountain lake
  b [ ] her favourite shopping centre
  c [ ] some famous places

5 What would Katia's dream home be?
  a [ ] an apartment
  b [ ] a cottage
  c [ ] a palace

6 What size would Katia's dream home be?
  a [ ] small and cosy
  b [ ] medium-sized
  c [ ] very large

7 Where would Katia like to have picnics and parties?
  a [ ] in Pushkin Square
  b [ ] on her balcony
  c [ ] in her kitchen

8 What kind of kitchen would she like to have?
  a [ ] a kitchen with gold tables and chairs
  b [ ] a modern kitchen with lots of technology
  c [ ] an old-fashioned kitchen

c Write about your dream home. Remember to include:
- the location
- the views
- the size / number of rooms
- the type of home
- what the building looks like.

◉ Review and extension

1 GRAMMAR

Correct the sentences.

1 He isn't answering the phone so he must to be away on holiday.
  He isn't answering the phone so he must be away on holiday.
2 George isn't enough good at football to play for the school team.
3 She mustn't be the manager – she looks too young!
4 There's much traffic in the town centre during the rush hour.
5 They mustn't be doing their homework at this moment – it's nearly midnight!
6 The maths exam was too much difficult for most of the people in my class.

2 VOCABULARY

Correct the sentences.

1 His new flat is in an excellent place. There's a beautiful park opposite and the metro station's only 200 metres away.
  His new flat is in an excellent location. There's a beautiful park opposite and the metro station's only 200 metres away.
2 She complainted to the waiter about the dirty glass.
3 I can't afford to buy a flat at the moment so I'm going to hire a flat in the city centre.
4 Don't worry about the bill. I'll pay the meal.
5 I live in a really nice neighbour – everyone's very friendly.
6 When he told me about the accident, I didn't believe in him at first.

3 WORDPOWER *over*

Match 1–6 with a–f to make sentences.

1 [b] I've only seen her three or four times over
2 [ ] After about three minutes, turn the steak over
3 [ ] It usually takes about seven hours to fly over
4 [ ] If the match starts at 3 o'clock, it should be over
5 [ ] By 2050 there will be over
6 [ ] There's glass all over

a the Atlantic from New York to London.
b the past 20 years.
c and cook the other side.
d the floor because I dropped a vase.
e 10 billion people living on the planet.
f by a quarter to five.

◔ REVIEW YOUR PROGRESS

Look again at Review your progress on p.90 of the Student's Book. How well can you do these things now?
3 = very well   2 = well   1 = not so well

I CAN …

describe a building	[ ]
describe a town or city	[ ]
make offers and ask for permission	[ ]
write a note with useful information.	[ ]

1 GRAMMAR Reported speech: statements and questions

a Correct the mistakes in the sentences with reported speech. There may be more than one mistake in each sentence.

1 Yesterday John said, 'I'm going to phone my mother this evening.'
Yesterday John said me that he's going to phone my mother this evening.
Yesterday John told me that he was going to phone his mother that evening.

2 'You should wait behind this line until it is your turn.'
She said I should wait behind this line until it is your turn.

_____

3 'Are you going to Harry's party tomorrow?'
When I met her last Friday she asked to me if I'm going to Harry's party tomorrow.

_____

4 'He might be about fifty years old.'
She said me he might be about fifty years old.

_____

5 He said, 'I'm sorry but I can't come to your party this evening.'
He told he's sorry but he can't come to my party this evening.

_____

6 'Did you see your uncle when you were in New York last year?'
She asked me did I see your uncle when I were in New York last year.

_____

7 'Goodbye, Anna. I'll see you next week.'
He told Anna he will see me next week.

_____

b Complete the reported speech with the correct verb form. Change the tense where possible.

1 'Mandy's coming to stay with me next week.'
She said that _Mandy was coming to stay with her the following week._

2 'Martin has just sent me a text message.'
He said that _____.

3 'I'll phone you when I get home from work.'
He told me _____.

4 'Are you going to buy your brother a present this afternoon?'
He asked me _____.

5 'Why can't you lend me some money?'
She asked me _____.

6 'You must stop writing immediately and give me your papers.'
The examiner said that we

_____

7 'I want you to take these flowers for your grandmother.'
She told me _____.

2 VOCABULARY The news

a Underline the correct words to complete the sentences.

1 The *reporter* / *editor* / *presenter* is the most important journalist at a newspaper.

2 Let's listen to the *notices* / *journals* / *news* on the radio to see if they say anything about tomorrow's underground drivers' strike.

3 If you want to know what's happening in Hollywood, you should watch the *business* / *entertainment* / *political* news.

4 News of the explosion in Washington *posted* / *communicated* / *spread* very quickly on Facebook.

5 My newspaper has four pages of *current affairs* / *celebrity gossip* / *feeds* about the lives of Hollywood actors and sports stars.

6 He's a billionaire who owns the biggest news *company* / *feed* / *organisation* in Europe.

7 There's a *current* / *news* / *politics* affairs programme on TV tonight about the presidential elections in the USA.

8 I want to watch the *entertainment* / *political* / *business* news because I'm interested in next week's local elections.

b Complete the crossword puzzle.

→ **Across**

4 Most companies advertise their products on social ____media____ like Facebook and Twitter.

6 She's going to be the new _____ of *The X Factor* on Channel 6.

7 Have you heard the _____ news about the accident on the motorway?

8 He _____ a comment about the concert on Facebook five minutes after it finished.

↓ **Down**

1 When she saw the _____ TRAIN CRASH DISASTER, she immediately called her husband to make sure he was all right.

2 He wrote a fascinating _____ in *The Times* about the problems of air pollution in London.

3 The local TV station sent their sports _____ to interview the new manager of the town's football team.

5 In the _____ news section of the newspaper there was an interesting article about the economic crisis.

1 GRAMMAR Verb patterns

a Complete the sentences with the *-ing* form or the *to +* infinitive form of the verb in brackets.

1 __*Reading*__ (read) a good book is an excellent way to relax before _____ (go) to bed.
2 She remembered _____ (see) the film in the cinema when she was a little girl.
3 It will be extremely difficult _____ (get) a ticket for the World Cup Final.
4 We promised _____ (come) back at the same time the following day.
5 He didn't enjoy _____ (visit) his grandparents.
6 Would you mind _____ (wait) here for me while I get changed?
7 Instead of _____ (go) to the bookshop they went to the library _____ (see) if they could borrow a copy of *Oliver Twist*.
8 In my view it isn't worth _____ (pay) to see the new Spielberg film.

b Correct the sentences.

1 I phoned Philip ask him if he wanted playing tennis at the weekend.
   I phoned Philip to ask him if he wanted to play tennis
   at the weekend.
2 Don't forget giving me back my book when you've finished read it.
   _____
3 He admitted to steal the old lady's handbag.
   _____
4 We hoped finding a good place to eat in one of the streets near the station.
   _____
5 He threatened telling my parents what I had done.
   _____
6 It's really important teach your children how crossing the road safely.
   _____
7 She didn't know which book buying her brother for his birthday.
   _____
8 You promised helping me with my homework!
   _____

2 VOCABULARY Shopping

a Complete the conversation with the words in the box.

| sale bargain refund priced |
| ~~browsing~~ come back afford value |

SHOP ASSISTANT	Good morning. Can I help you?
CUSTOMER 1	No, thank you. I'm just [1] __*browsing*__.
CUSTOMER 2	So what kind of present do you want to buy for your nephew?
CUSTOMER 1	I'm not really sure.
CUSTOMER 2	It's difficult, isn't it? Let's have a look in the computer games section. I think they said on the radio that 'Mayhem 5' was going to [2] _____ out this week.
CUSTOMER 1	Yes, I think I heard that, too. Let's see if it's on [3] _____.
CUSTOMER 2	Look, there it is. €49.90.
CUSTOMER 1	49.90! I can't [4] _____ that!
CUSTOMER 2	You're right. That's a lot of money for a computer game. Let's have a look at the special offers over there. Here's one that's reasonably [5] _____. It's from last year and it's only €19.99. That's a [6] _____, isn't it?
CUSTOMER 1	Yes, that's good [7] _____ for money. I'll buy him that one. I hope he doesn't already have it.
SHOP ASSISTANT	Don't worry. He can always take it [8] _____ to his local store and change it for another one or get a [9] _____.
CUSTOMER 1	OK, that's great. I'll take it, then.

b ▶ **8.1** Listen and check.

3 VOCABULARY Reporting verbs

a Complete the sentences with the correct form of the verbs in the box.

| warn ~~advise~~ refuse offer agree suggest |

1 'You should apply for the Head of Marketing job.'
   He __*advised*__ her to apply for the Head of Marketing job.
2 'Yes, that's fine. I'm happy to sell you my car for £5,000.'
   She _____ to sell me her car for £5,000.
3 'Why don't we go to the beach tomorrow?'
   He _____ going to the beach the following day.
4 'Be careful! Don't touch that plate – it's hot!'
   He _____ her not to touch the plate as it was hot.
5 'I'm not going to lend you any more money.'
   I _____ to lend her any more money.
6 'If you like, I can give you a lift to the station.'
   He _____ to give us a lift to the station.

8C Everyday English
On the whole, I prefer taking action shots

1 USEFUL LANGUAGE
Generalising

a Put the words in the right order to make sentences.

1 be / film / of / honest, / the / was / boring / kind / to .
   To be honest, the film was kind of boring.

2 my / tend / Americans / be / experience, / friendly / to / very / in .
   _____

3 normally / that / thing / of / I / like / kind / don't .
   _____

4 whole, / I / his / liked / film / the / new / on .
   _____

5 songs / of / his / can / depressing / some / rather / be .
   _____

6 a / coffee / Italian / is / rule, / excellent / as .
   _____

b ⏵**8.2** Listen and check.

2 CONVERSATION SKILLS Being vague

a Complete the sentences with the words in the box.

| whole | stuff | ~~that~~ | couple | sort |

1 He likes hip hop and rap music – you know, stuff like ____that____.

2 We had a _____ of days when it was cloudy and rainy, but on the _____ we had pretty good weather.

3 Don't touch all that _____ in his office, please.

4 She likes watching documentaries about animals and nature and that _____ of thing.

b ⏵**8.3** Listen and check.

3 PRONUNCIATION
Sound and spelling: /h/ and /w/

a ⏵**8.4** Listen to the sentences. Put the words in **bold** in the correct columns.

1 **When** did you last see her?
2 They **went** the **wrong way** and got lost.
3 **Whose** suitcase was the **heaviest**?
4 I **wrote** a long letter to my uncle in Scotland.
5 I didn't know **which** book to get my **husband**.
6 She **had** to wait two **hours** for the next train to London.

Sound 1 /h/ (e.g. *h*ot)	Sound 2 /w/ (e.g. *w*ith)	First letter silent (e.g. *h*onest)

b ⏵**8.5** Listen and check.

1 READING

a Read the email and tick (✓) the correct answer.

a ☐ The alligator attacked Blackie and broke his leg.
b ☐ The alligator bit Pam and broke her leg.
c ☐ Blackie was afraid of the alligator and didn't stay with Pam.
d ☐ Pam broke her leg while she was walking with Blackie.

I read an amazing story in the newspaper this morning about a dog called Blackie who saved his owner's life in Florida. It seems that his owner, Pam Evans, who is 79 years old, was walking near a lake when she fell over and broke her leg. Unfortunately, she couldn't move and didn't have a mobile phone so she couldn't call for help. At that moment, a huge alligator came out of the lake and started walking towards Pam, threatening to attack her. Incredibly, Blackie wasn't frightened by the alligator and, apparently, he started fighting it to try and protect Pam. Amazingly, after a few minutes, the alligator gave up trying to attack Pam and went back into the lake. Fortunately, a man who was near the lake with his dog heard Blackie barking and came to rescue Pam. It seems that he then phoned for an ambulance, which immediately took Pam to hospital. Luckily, neither Pam nor Blackie were hurt in the attack and Pam has now made a full recovery.

b Read the news story again. Are the sentences true or false?

1 Pam Evans has a dog called Blackie.
2 Pam couldn't call for help because her mobile phone was broken.
3 When Blackie saw the alligator he was very frightened and ran away.
4 The man near the lake called for an ambulance.
5 Blackie was seriously injured by the alligator.

2 WRITING SKILLS
Summarising information

a Use one of the words in the box to connect the sentences. Make any necessary changes. Sometimes there is more than one possible answer.

before	who	but	with	and	which

1 The man spent several hours looking for his son. Unfortunately, he couldn't find him anywhere.
   The man spent several hours looking for his son but, unfortunately, he couldn't find him anywhere.

2 I heard a story on the radio about an elephant. Apparently, it sat on a car in a safari park.

3 The 12-year-old girl stole her father's motorbike. She rode it for 40 km along the motorway. The police stopped her near Oxford.

4 The woman hit the teenager hard on his head with her umbrella. Then she used his mobile phone to call the police.

5 Amanda escaped from the burning building by breaking a window. She used her shoe to break the window.

6 There was an incredible story on the news about a baby in China. She fell from a fourth-floor window. She wasn't hurt because a man in the street caught her.

3 WRITING

a Read the notes. Write the story.

FAMILY'S LUCKY ESCAPE WHEN CAR CRASHES INTO HOUSE

Car crashed into house. Manchester.
Family watching TV in living room at time of accident. Heard loud noise.
Driver lost control of car. Drove straight through front door. Stopped 2 metres from kitchen.
No-one seriously hurt. Driver & 3 passengers only minor injuries.
Police were called. Arrived 5 minutes later.
Front of house badly damaged.
Car removed. Took fire service 6 hours.

UNIT 8
Reading and listening extension

1 READING

a Read the article and tick (✓) the correct answers.

1 Why has the article been written?
   - a ☐ to encourage more students to take courses in journalism
   - b ☐ to explain why careers in journalism have become popular with students
   - c ☐ to show the advantages and disadvantages of a career in journalism

2 Who has the article been written for?
   - a ☐ owners of news organisations
   - b ☐ professional journalists
   - c ☐ students who study journalism

3 Which of these things do Mercedes and Frankie have in common?
   - a ☐ They both earn good money at their job.
   - b ☐ They both love their work.
   - c ☐ They both studied journalism at university.

4 Mercedes and Frankie both agree that people who want to become journalists …
   - a ☐ need to travel all over the world.
   - b ☐ should be really interested in journalism.
   - c ☐ will have to work at weekends.

b Read the text again and tick (✓) the correct answers.

Who …	Mercedes	Frankie	Neither Mercedes nor Frankie
1 works when they are travelling?	✓		
2 enjoys thinking about the readers of their stories?			
3 has a parent that was also a journalist?			
4 does not sleep very much?			
5 won a prize for journalism while at university?			
6 often writes more than one story in a day?			
7 always knew they wanted to be a journalist?			
8 became a journalist by accident?			
9 takes their own photos for their stories?			
10 has no free time in the mornings?			
11 works from home?			
12 writes stories of 1,000 words?			

c Read the notice from a student magazine. Write a short article.

We are looking for people to tell us about their experiences of work or study. We would like you to write a short article explaining:
- what your job is or what you are studying
- why you have chosen the job or course you are doing
- a typical day at work or at university.

CAREERS FOR LIFE

*A report this week announced that **journalism courses** are now more popular than ever with students. But what is it like to work as a journalist? Here, two young journalists tell Careers for Life about their experience.*

THE NEWSPAPER JOURNALIST
Mercedes Alvarado, 24

A typical day for me starts at 7 am. The morning is always the hardest part of the day because I have to work all the time without any breaks. I only have about 7 or 8 hours to finish a story and there is a lot to do in that time.

First, I have to interview people for the story and sometimes that means travelling quite a long way. I usually go by train so that I can carry on working on my laptop. I also need to think about photos for the story. These days I usually buy pictures from a photo agency but sometimes a photographer goes with me on a story. I usually have to write a story of about 1,000 words and it can be very difficult to do that in only a few hours. By 4 pm I'm usually exhausted, but I don't normally leave work until 5 pm.

I have wanted to be a journalist since I was five years old and I studied journalism at university, so working for a newspaper has been a dream come true. Journalism is a great career but can be a very stressful one that does not pay very well. Anyone who is thinking of becoming a journalist needs to know that.

THE BUSINESS BLOGGER
Frankie Kaufman, 20

I had never had any plans to become a journalist but then I started my business blog when I was still at university. I wasn't enjoying life as a student so when a news organisation offered to pay me for my reports I immediately accepted. I eventually quit university to blog full time, even though I've never actually had any training as a reporter.

My day starts at 4 am when I check Twitter in bed to find out what has happened around the world during the night. I start preparing my first report at around 4.30 am and it is usually finished and on my website by 5.30 am. In a normal day I can expect to write maybe five or six reports and I usually manage to sell at least two or three of them to news agencies. It's really exciting when an agency from another country buys one of my reports. I love the idea that something that I wrote in my kitchen is being read by someone in Dubai or Dallas.

I make good money but I work hard for it. I often don't go to bed until 11 pm and I usually work 7 days a week. I would say that unless you are really in love with journalism this is not a career for you.

2 LISTENING

a ▶ **8.6** Listen to a conversation between two friends, Cathy and Cindy. Are the sentences true or false?

1 One of the women bought a painting.
2 One of the women bought something that she is not happy with.
3 One of the women has been in an argument in a shop.
4 One of the women has bought a pair of boots.
5 One of the women has some good news.
6 One of the women is an artist.
7 One of the women is complaining about something.
8 One of the women is the manager of a shop.

b Listen to the conversation again and tick (✓) the correct answers.

1 When did Cathy buy the boots?
  a ☐ in the morning
  b ☐ yesterday
  c ☐ last week

2 Why did Cathy think the boots were 'good value'?
  a ☐ They were half price.
  b ☐ They were designer boots.
  c ☐ They only cost £50.

3 The problem was that Cathy was given …
  a ☐ boots that had been damaged.
  b ☐ boots of the wrong size.
  c ☐ boots in white instead of brown.

4 Cathy didn't notice the problem until later because the shop assistant …
  a ☐ didn't open the box for her.
  b ☐ hid the problem from her.
  c ☐ gave her the wrong box.

5 The manager of the shop …
  a ☐ offered to give Cathy another pair of boots.
  b ☐ promised to give Cathy a refund.
  c ☐ refused to give Cathy her money back.

6 What is Cathy going to do next?
  a ☐ She is going to call the police.
  b ☐ She is not sure what to do next.
  c ☐ She is going to sell the boots.

c Write a conversation between two people who are Cathy's friends. Person A tells Person B what happened to Cathy; Person B asks questions. Listen to the conversation again and make notes to help you retell the story.

⊙ Review and extension

1 GRAMMAR

Correct the sentences.

1 She said me she didn't like horror films.
  She told me she didn't like horror films.
2 They asked me was I going to the football match.
3 He has agreed taking us to the airport.
4 When I phoned him last night, he said he has just finished his exams.
5 She advised me not tell anyone about our meeting.
6 Yesterday he told he would help me with my homework.
7 I'm really looking forward to see you on Sunday.

2 VOCABULARY

Correct the sentences.

1 I was shocked when I heard the notices on the radio about the explosion.
  I was shocked when I heard the news on the radio about the explosion.
2 The new song by Rihanna is going to come across next week.
3 My sister likes reading the celebrity gossips pages in the Sunday paper.
4 He adviced me to buy a new laptop because mine is over five years old.
5 I don't usually watch programmes about politic on TV.
6 She remembered me to book a table at the restaurant.
7 The main title on the front page of my newspaper today is BARACK WINS U.S. ELECTION.

3 WORDPOWER *in/on* + noun

Underline the correct words to complete the sentences.

1 There are some beautiful photos of Venice *in* / *on* this magazine.
2 I sent him a message *in* / *on* Facebook but he hasn't replied yet.
3 It's better to watch this film *in* / *on* a big screen at the cinema.
4 You always look so pretty *in* / *on* photos!
5 There's always an easy crossword *in* / *on* my newspaper.
6 Is there anything good *in* / *on* TV tonight?
7 Can you pay me *in* / *on* US dollars, please?
8 Do you have this T-shirt *in* / *on* a large size, please?

⟳ REVIEW YOUR PROGRESS

Look again at Review your progress on p.102 of the Student's Book. How well can you do these things now?
3 = very well   2 = well   1 = not so well

I CAN …

talk about the news	☐
talk about what other people say	☐
generalise and be vague	☐
write an email summary of a news story.	☐

9A The film is still loved today

1 GRAMMAR The passive

a Put the words in the correct order to make passive sentences.

1 3D cameras / new / will / *Star Wars* / the / filmed / movie / be / with .
The new Star Wars movie will be filmed with 3D cameras.

2 by / directed / Steven Spielberg / was / in / *Saving Private Ryan* / 1998 .
_____

3 the / been / come / have / told / to / at / back / 15.00 / actors .
_____

4 every / are / films / made / Bollywood / year / in / 1,000 .
_____

5 seen / 35 million / was / in / people / its first two weeks / by / the movie *Avatar* .
_____

6 interviewed / on / this very moment / the / being / TV / at / prime minister / is .
_____

7 cars / every / 200,000 / produced / new factory / year / by / are / our .
_____

8 special effects / is / create / used / the / CGI / being / to .
_____

b Rewrite the sentences. Use the passive.

1 They built 250,000 new houses each year in the 1990s.
250,000 new houses were built each year in the 1990s.

2 They grow five different varieties of orange in this region.
Five _____

3 The government will give students a loan to pay for their university fees.
Students _____

4 They are creating the special effects with the latest animation software.
The special effects _____

5 They've asked the actors to give some of their fees to charity.
The actors _____

6 He was driving the car really fast when the accident happened.
The car _____

7 The journalist asked the pop star about his new album.
The pop star _____

8 A little girl in a pink dress gave the president a big bunch of flowers.
The president _____

2 VOCABULARY Cinema and TV

a Complete the sentences with the words in the box.

~~drama~~   chat show   horror   action   thriller   game show
documentary   science fiction   soap opera   animated

1 *Captain Phillips* is a ____drama____ starring Tom Hanks about an American boat that is hijacked by Somali pirates.

2 *Dracula* is one of the most famous _____ films of all time.

3 I saw a really exciting _____ at the cinema on Saturday. It was about a detective who was trying to prevent a gang from stealing a famous painting from the National Gallery.

4 I'm not very keen on _____ _____ films like *Star Wars* or *The Matrix*.

5 My friend was on the _____ _____ *Who Wants to Be a Millionaire?* and won £5,000!

6 There was a fascinating wildlife _____ on TV last night about African elephants.

7 I think *Shrek* is one of the best _____ films for children I've ever seen.

8 They had some brilliant guests on that _____ _____ on Channel 4: Brad Pitt and Lady Gaga!

9 I love _____ films like *Mission: Impossible* and the James Bond series.

10 *EastEnders* is a very popular _____ _____ on British TV about the everyday lives of a group of people who live in the East End of London.

b Complete the crossword puzzle.

```
                              ┌─┐
                              │1│
                          ┌─┬─┼─┼─┐
                         2│F│I│L│M│
                          └─┴─┼─┼─┘
                    ┌─┐       │ │
                   3│ │       │ │
                 ┌─┼─┼─┬─┬─┬─┬─┼─┐
                4│ │ │ │ │ │ │ │ │
                 └─┼─┼─┴─┴─┴─┴─┼─┘
                   │ │         │ │
                   │ │         │ │
        ┌─┐        │ │         │ │
       5│ │ │ │ │ │ │ │ │
        └─┴─┴─┴─┴─┴─┴─┴─┘
```

→ **Across**

2 It took six months to ____film____ *Titanic* and it cost over $200 million to make.

4 In *The Curious Case of Benjamin Button*, Brad Pitt plays a _____ who gets younger and younger as the film progresses.

5 The film *Romeo and Juliet* stars Leonardo DiCaprio and Claire Danes, and is _____ _____ the famous play by William Shakespeare.

↓ **Down**

1 The _____ is the person who gives instructions to the actors and takes all the important decisions when a film is being made.

3 In my opinion, the best _____ in the film is when Paul and Sarah meet again after 25 years.

9B I went to a concert which changed my life

1 GRAMMAR Defining and non-defining relative clauses

a Rewrite the sentences. Use the information in brackets as a non-defining relative clause.

1 The opera singer gave us some free tickets for her concert. (Her husband is a famous author.)
   The opera singer, whose husband is a famous author,
   gave us some free tickets for her concert.

2 While you're in Italy you should visit the town of Verona. (There is a lovely Roman amphitheatre in Verona.)

3 John Lennon was murdered in 1980. (He was a member of the pop group The Beatles.)

4 Pelé was a famous Brazilian footballer. (His real name is Edson Arantes do Nascimento.)

5 Steven Spielberg was the director of the film *Saving Private Ryan*. (It was about a group of American soldiers in the Second World War.)

6 First we went to Paris and then we took the train to Lyon. (In Paris we visited the Eiffel Tower.)

7 In my view, Bruce Springsteen's best album is *The River*. (He recorded it in 1980.)

8 Bill Clinton is giving a talk at our university next month. (He was President of the USA from 1993 to 2001.)

2 VOCABULARY Music

a Complete the words in the text.

① When I was in London last summer I went to a superb concert during the BBC Proms, which is a ¹f_estival_____ of classical music at the Royal Albert Hall. It's great to hear a symphony or a concerto when it's ²p_____ by an ³o_____ of professional ⁴m_____ who are playing ⁵l_____ They played symphonies by Mahler and Beethoven and there was also a huge ⁶c_____ of 80 people that sang Mozart's Requiem. At the end of the concert everyone in the ⁷a_____ stood up and gave the performers a standing ovation which lasted for over five minutes.

② I've just heard on the radio that the band have been in the ⁸r_____ studio for the last month. They're making a new ⁹a_____ of jazz, soul and blues songs, which they're bringing out in September. I've just listened to an amazing ¹⁰p_____ of their old songs on the Internet. It's got about 30 ¹¹t_____ on it and most of them are old songs of theirs from the 80s and 90s.

b ▶9.1 Listen and check.

3 VOCABULARY Word-building: nouns

a Complete the sentences with the noun forms of the words in brackets.

1 Lots of writers have tried to describe the ___beauty___ (beautiful) of the Taj Mahal in India.
2 My football team gave its best _____ (perform) of the season and won the match 4 – 0.
3 He has donated £100 to a _____ (charitable) that is providing schools for poor villages in Africa.
4 We believe that staff _____ (develop) is very important so we provide regular training courses for all of our employees.
5 In my view, money can't buy you _____ (happy).
6 You need plenty of _____ (creative) to write good children's stories.
7 There will be a huge _____ (celebrate) in Edinburgh this New Year's Eve, with live performances by bands and a big fireworks display.
8 There is a fascinating exhibition of Aztec art and _____ (cultural) at the British Museum at the moment.

4 PRONUNCIATION Defining and non-defining relative clauses

a ▶9.2 Listen to the sentences. Is the relative clause defining or non-defining? Tick (✓) the correct box.

	Defining	Non-defining
1 … which have a lot of adverts …	✓	
2 … which they recorded in 2010 …		
3 … whose brother is also a musician …		
4 … who eat healthily…		
5 … which my sister went to …		
6 … which last more than three hours …		

9C Everyday English
It's meant to be excellent

1 USEFUL LANGUAGE
Recommending and responding

a <u>Underline</u> the correct words to complete the conversation.

PAM Hi, Mel. Listen. Ian and I were thinking of [1]*go / going* out for a meal this weekend. [2]*Do / Would* you guys like to [3]*come / coming* with us?

MEL Yes, [4]*it's / that's* a great idea. Where were you planning [5]*going / to go*?

PAM We [6]*think / thought* about going to that new Chinese restaurant in town. It's [7]*meaning / meant* to be really good.

MEL [8]*Hang / Wait* on a second. I'll just ask Tony … Sorry, Pam, but Tony isn't a big fan [9]*from / of* Chinese food.

PAM OK, never mind. We could go somewhere [10]*other / else*.

MEL Oh, I know. How about [11]*go / going* to that new Italian restaurant near the station?

PAM Mmm, that [12]*seems / sounds* interesting.

MEL Yes, it's [13]*supposed / suggested* to be excellent, and very good value for money.

PAM Yes, I'm sure Ian [14]*likes / would like* it. He loves pizzas and pasta.

MEL Good. [15]*Shall / Will* I book a table for Saturday evening?

PAM Yes, that would be perfect for us. Why [16]*won't / don't* we get a table for 8 o'clock?

MEL Yes, OK. I'll book one.

b ▶9.3 Listen and check.

c Complete the words.

1 Sorry, but Sean isn't a big f<u>an</u> of science fiction films. What other films are on?

2 The new novel by JK Rowling, who wrote the Harry Potter books, is s_____ to be really good.

3 The new animated film from Pixar has had great r_____ in the papers.

4 **A** There's a documentary about the Roman occupation of Britain on TV tonight.
   B Really? That s_____ interesting.

5 I'm not s_____ my father would be i_____ in going to an exhibition of surrealist paintings.

6 This hotel was r_____ by a friend of mine, who stayed here last year.

7 That's a great i_____. I'm sure Andy would l_____ it.

8 The new Greek restaurant near my house is m_____ to be very good.

d ▶9.4 Listen and check.

2 PRONUNCIATION
Showing contrast

a ▶9.5 Listen to the exchanges. <u>Underline</u> the word or words which are stressed in the responses.

1 **A** Did you go to the concert with Luke?
   B No, I went with Will.

2 **A** Did James go to Edinburgh by bus?
   B No, he went on the train.

3 **A** So, your friend's a famous actor?
   B No, she's a famous dancer.

4 **A** So, you're from Lecce, in the south of Italy?
   B No, I'm from Lecco, in the north of Italy.

5 **A** Are you meeting your friend Pam on Thursday?
   B No, I'm meeting my friend Sam, on Tuesday.

D Skills for Writing

I like going out, but …

1 READING

a Read the text and tick (✓) the correct answer.

Mike likes watching sport on TV because …

a ☐ he can't see the players when he is in the stadium.
b ☐ it's less expensive than going to the stadium.
c ☐ it's dangerous to go to the stadium.
d ☐ it's more exciting to watch the match at home.

b Read the text again. Are the sentences true or false?

1 Everyone in Mike's family likes watching their local team.
2 The sports channels that show live football matches are free.
3 It is easier to see what is happening when you are in the stadium.
4 The TV commentator tells you lots of interesting things about the players.
5 Mike doesn't like being in a huge stadium with thousands of other people.

2 WRITING SKILLS Contrasting ideas

a Underline the correct words to complete the sentences.

1 I enjoyed seeing the new film *Julius Caesar* at the cinema, *although* / *in spite of* / *while* the noisy family who were sitting behind me.
2 *However* / *Despite* / *Although* I generally enjoy science fiction films, I wouldn't recommend the film *Black Hole*.
3 Steven Spielberg is a great director. *However* / *While* / *Although*, I thought his last film was actually rather boring.
4 *However* / *Although* / *Despite* the loud rock music that accompanied most of the action scenes, I really enjoyed the film.
5 *Despite* / *While* / *However* I agree with you that George Clooney is a good actor, I think he's mainly famous because of his looks.
6 *Although* / *Despite* / *However* it's more convenient to download movies from the Internet, more and more people are watching films at their local cinemas.
7 *Despite* / *While* / *Although* the superb acting and the exciting action scenes, I thought the film was too long and rather boring.
8 *While* / *However* / *In spite of* the amazing special effects, I wouldn't recommend seeing that film because the story wasn't very interesting.

Why I prefer watching sport on TV
by Mike Adams

I love all kinds of sport, especially football, rugby and tennis. However, I prefer watching it live on TV instead of going to the stadium.

The first reason for staying at home to watch sport is the cost. Although my whole family are big fans of our local football team, I can't afford to pay for four tickets to watch a match at the stadium every two weeks. While I have to pay extra to get the sports channels which show live football matches every week, it is much cheaper than going to the stadium.

Another reason I prefer watching sport live on TV is that you get a better view of the action. In a stadium the spectators are not usually very close to the players so it is sometimes difficult to see everything that happens clearly. Furthermore, on TV they show you the action from lots of different angles and they replay the most important parts of the match again and again. And when you watch a match on TV the commentator explains what is happening and gives you lots of interesting information about the players and the teams, which you don't get when you're watching in the stadium.

Finally, I don't enjoy being in a place where there are 50,000 other people. It's true that these days football stadiums are very safe places to watch matches. However, I sometimes get claustrophobic when I'm in a big crowd of people so it's much better to be at home, where I can watch a match with my family or just a few friends.

So, although watching a match on TV probably isn't as exciting as being in the stadium, I generally prefer watching sport live on TV. It's cheaper, I can see the action more easily and I can share the experience with my family and friends.

3 WRITING

a Read the notes. Write an article explaining why you prefer reading the original book rather than a film which has been adapted from a book.

Why I prefer reading a book
Paragraph 1
• Introduction: State your position.
Paragraph 2
• Longer to read a book than watch a film. More enjoyment from books.
• Interesting details often cut from films.
Paragraph 3
• Need to use your imagination when reading a story.
• In films, director decides appearance of people and places, not you.
Paragraph 4
• Books a great way to relax. Can enter a world that author created.
• Can read a book anywhere. Very convenient.
Paragraph 5
• Conclusion: Repeat the main points.

UNIT 9
Reading and listening extension

1 READING

a Read the text. Are the sentences true or false?

1 The main topic of the text is Marc Boulanger.
2 Marc Boulanger knows a lot about popular African music.
3 Marc Boulanger is from France.
4 Konono N°1 is the name of a music festival.
5 'Tommo23' is interested in what Marc Boulanger wrote.
6 'ShSh41' agrees with Marc Boulanger.

b Read the text again and tick (✓) the correct answer.

1 Why was Konono N°1's concert so interesting for Marc?
  a ☐ because Fela Kuti had recommended the band to him
  b ☐ because he had never visited Paris before
  c ☐ because it was the first time he had ever heard popular African music
  d ☐ because their music was not similar to anything else he knew

2 Who used to make traditional instruments out of elephant tusks?
  a ☐ Fela Kuti
  b ☐ Kanda Bongo Man
  c ☐ People from Angola
  d ☐ The Bazombo people

3 What is a *likembé*?
  a ☐ a kind of elephant
  b ☐ a kind of instrument
  c ☐ a kind of musician
  d ☐ a kind of sound

4 All the instruments used by Konono N°1 have been made by hand …
  a ☐ apart from the instruments they found in the street.
  b ☐ except the electric instruments, which they bought.
  c ☐ including all the electric instruments which they use.
  d ☐ except for the piano and drums.

5 According to 'ShSh41', who combined music with politics?
  a ☐ Fela Kuti
  b ☐ Kanda Bongo Man
  c ☐ Konono N°1
  d ☐ Mawangu Mingiedi

c You are going to write a blog for *Heroes of Music*. First, make notes about a singer, musician or band whose music you like very much. Use the Internet to help you make notes about:

- the name of the singer/musician/band
- the history of the singer/musician/band
- any interesting details about the singer/musician/band

HEROES OF MUSIC

<u>Marc Boulanger</u>, on the sweet sounds of Congolese band, <u>Konono N°1</u>:

I was just 15 when I saw Konono N°1 perform live. They were playing a concert in Paris, my hometown, and although I had been serious about playing music since the age of 10, I had never seen or heard anything like this band before. I don't mean that I had never heard any popular African music before. Even at 15, I had already heard of musicians such as Fela Kuti and Kanda Bongo Man. So what was different about this folk orchestra?

First of all, I think it is the way that they mix modern culture with the cultural traditions of the Bazombo people, who live near the border with Angola. In that ancient tradition, musical instruments were made out of elephant tusks*. But Mawangu Mingiedi, the musician who started Konono N°1, introduced electric *likembé* (a traditional *likembé* is part piano, part drum). They have a really special sound – they have a beauty which you just won't hear anywhere else.

Secondly, the instruments they use are really interesting. Every one of them has been made out of old bits of wood and metal and other rubbish that they have found just lying around. Even the electric instruments that they use have been made using batteries from old cars and broken lamps as well as small magnets. Again, this all helps to create a sound that is unlike anything else you might hear.

Finally, there is the amazing rhythm they use. Every time I listen to it I get a really strong feeling of excitement. Everyone who hears that beat is filled with so much happiness that they just have to start dancing.

 COMMENTS

 Posted by: Tommo23 09:13

Thanks for this. I've just read Marc's full article. Really great story. They're going to do a performance at this year's Edinburgh festival in August. I can't wait to go.

 Posted by: ShSh41 10:23

Yeah, I don't know. In spite of my love of African music I think there are other bands who are more important than these guys. Fela Kuti is just the best. Now there was a guy who managed to put music and politics together. Definitely a hero for me.

Review and extension

1 GRAMMAR

Correct the sentences.

1 *Romeo and Juliet* is written from Shakespeare.
   Romeo and Juliet was written by Shakespeare.
2 A new bridge is built at the moment with a Chinese construction company.
3 I interviewed the actor which had just won an Oscar.
4 *Sunflowers* was painted from Vincent Van Gogh.
5 Where the new James Bond film being made?
6 He's the player used to be in our team.

2 LISTENING

a ▶9.6 Listen to three people talking and tick (✓) the correct answers.

1 The speakers must be …
   a ☐ at a local cinema.
   b ☐ at someone's house.
   c ☐ in a classroom.
2 The speakers are trying to decide …
   a ☐ what to buy.
   b ☐ what to eat.
   c ☐ what to watch.
3 Which type of film do the women not want to watch?
   a ☐ comedy
   b ☐ documentary
   c ☐ science fiction
4 Which type of film do they all agree to watch?
   a ☐ comedy
   b ☐ documentary
   c ☐ science fiction

b Listen again. Complete the sentences with the words you hear in the conversation.

1 The man says he remembered to order a __vegetarian__ pizza.
2 They are going to watch the films on the _____.
3 *Blackfish* is the name of a _____ film.
4 The man thinks the film *Blackfish* will probably be quite _____ .
5 According to one of the women, the film *Man on the Moon* has amazing _____, beautiful photography and a great story.
6 The man does not think that *Man on the Moon* is a _____ .
7 The film they all agree to watch is an _____ film.

c Write about the kind of films you like. Think about these questions:

• Do you think animated films are only for children? Why / Why not?
• If you could direct a film, what type of film would you most like to direct? Why?
• Which book would you most like to be made into a film? Why?

2 VOCABULARY

Correct the sentences.

1 There was a brilliant documentation about the Antarctic on TV last night.
   There was a brilliant documentary about the Antarctic on TV last night.
2 The actor was annoyed because someone in the crowd had forgotten to switch off his mobile phone.
3 My father's a professional music who plays the clarinet in the London Philharmonic Orchestra.
4 In *Titanic*, Leonardo DiCaprio plays a personality who falls in love with the daughter of an American millionaire.
5 When I was about sixteen I saw The Rolling Stones play life at a festival in Germany.
6 I'm not very keen on terror films like *Dracula*.

3 WORDPOWER
see, look at, watch, hear, listen to

Correct the sentences. Use the correct form of the verbs *see*, *look (at)*, *watch*, *hear*, or *listen (to)*.

1 Why don't we see the match on TV at your house?
   Why don't we watch the match on TV at your house?
2 Have you watched my brother? He said he'd meet me here.
3 I don't hear why you're so angry with us.
4 She always hears pop music in her bedroom.
5 I'm looking at my grandparents next Sunday.
6 Sorry, this phone's terrible. I can't listen to you very well.
7 I've finished this exercise. Please see it for me.

↻ REVIEW YOUR PROGRESS

Look again at Review your progress on p.114 of the Student's Book. How well can you do these things now?
3 = very well   2 = well   1 = not so well

I CAN …

talk about films and TV	☐
give extra information	☐
recommend and respond to recommendations	☐
write an article.	☐

1 GRAMMAR Second conditional

a Complete the sentences with the correct forms of the verbs in brackets. Use contractions where possible.

1 If you ___weren't___ (not be) so busy, you _____ (can) train to run a marathon.
2 I _____ (take) my daughter to the match if she _____ (be) interested in football.
3 I _____ (go) to the theatre at least once a month if I _____ (live) in London.
4 If I _____ (speak) Spanish, I _____ (apply) for a job in Madrid.
5 I'm sure you _____ (like) her if you _____ (know) her better.
6 I _____ (learn) another foreign language if I _____ (not have) so much work at the moment.
7 My sister _____ (buy) a new car if she _____ (can) afford it.
8 Germany don't have a very strong team at the moment, so I _____ (not be) surprised if England _____ (beat) them tomorrow.

b Decide if the first or second conditional is more suitable for each situation. Complete the sentences using the correct form of the verbs in the box. Use contractions where possible.

be (x3) have not live visit come
~~pass~~ train pay not lose finish

1 You've studied really hard this year. If you ___pass___ your exams, I _____ for your holiday to the USA.
2 He never goes to football training. If he _____ every day, he _____ a much better player.
3 Our team has won its last 10 matches. If we _____ our next match, we _____ champions again.
4 My current salary isn't very high. I _____ able to afford to buy a house if I _____ a job with a better salary.
5 Unfortunately, I live over 250 kilometres from my parents' house. If I _____ so far away, I _____ them more often.
6 I've nearly done all my homework. I _____ and watch the match at your house if I _____ it before nine o'clock.

2 VOCABULARY Sport

a Underline the correct words to complete the sentences.

1 If your *competitor* / <u>*opponent*</u> / *referee* doesn't return the ball, you *miss* / *beat* / *score* a point.
2 No, I didn't enjoy the cup final. My team *lost* / *beat* / *missed* the match 2 – 0.
3 We *didn't win* / *didn't beat* / *didn't score* the match because you *lost* / *missed* / *attacked* that penalty.
4 The last time we played tennis together, I *won* / *lost* / *beat* you easily.
5 If you love swimming in the sea, perhaps you should *have a go* / *compete* / *win* at scuba diving?
6 A standard athletics *court* / *pitch* / *track* has eight lanes and each lap is 400 metres.

3 VOCABULARY
Adjectives and prepositions

a Complete the sentences with one word from each box.

essential ~~proud~~ scared similar worried interested go

of (x2) for to in about at

1 That was the day my son won his gold medal. I was so ___proud___ ___of___ him.
2 Plenty of exercise and a good diet are _____ _____ a healthy lifestyle.
3 I'm not very _____ _____ current affairs.
4 I'm not very _____ _____ skiing. I love it but I always fall over and I have to go on the easiest slopes!
5 I think Portuguese is very _____ _____ Spanish.
6 My son hasn't done enough work so he's really _____ _____ his exams.
7 She didn't want to go to the top of the Eiffel Tower because she was _____ _____ heights.

4 PRONUNCIATION
Strong and weak forms: *would*

a ▶10.1 Listen to the pronunciation of *would* in these sentences. Is it strong (stressed) or weak (not stressed)? Write S (strong) or W (weak).

1 [W] I **would** go to the gym more often.
2 [ ] **A Would** he apply for a job in London?
  [ ] **B** No, he **wouldn't**.
3 [ ] She **wouldn't** lend you any money.
4 [ ] You **wouldn't** enjoy that film – it's too scary.
5 [ ] **A Would** you like to go for a pizza?
  [ ] **B** Yes, I **would**.

0B Making the most of opportunities

1 GRAMMAR Third conditional

a Underline the correct words to complete the sentences.

1 She *had won* / *might have won* / *would win* the gold medal if she *hadn't fallen* / *didn't fall* / *wouldn't have fallen* over at the start.

2 I *wouldn't have been able to* / *couldn't* / *hadn't been able to* get back into my house if I *would've lost* / *I've lost* / *I'd lost* my keys.

3 She *hadn't married* / *wouldn't have married* / *didn't marry* him if *she would've known* / *she knew* / *she'd known* that he'd been in prison.

4 If she *hadn't* / *wouldn't have* / *hasn't* helped him so much, he *mightn't have* / *hadn't* / *won't have* passed his exams.

5 We *hadn't* / *wouldn't have* / *won't have* got lost if you *hadn't* / *wouldn't have* / *had* forgotten to bring the map.

6 If she *wouldn't read* / *didn't read* / *hadn't read* that letter, she *didn't find* / *wouldn't have found* / *hadn't found* out about her family in Russia.

7 They *would have won* / *had won* / *would win* the match if their captain *didn't miss* / *hadn't missed* / *wouldn't miss* that penalty!

8 If it *didn't start* / *hadn't started* / *wouldn't have started* raining, we *had finished* / *would finish* / *could have finished* our game of tennis.

b Complete the text with the third conditional form of the verbs in brackets. Use contractions where possible.

This is the story of how I met my wife Jane. It all started when I was going to work by taxi and it suddenly broke down. If my taxi ¹ _hadn't broken_ (not/break) down, I ² _____ (get) to the station on time. If I ³ _____ (arrive) at the station on time, I ⁴ _____ (not/miss) my train. If I ⁵ _____ (not/miss) the train, I ⁶ _____ (not/have to) wait an hour for the next one. If I ⁷ _____ (not/have to) wait for an hour, I ⁸ _____ (not/go) to the café for a coffee. If I ⁹ _____ (not/have) a coffee, I ¹⁰ _____ (not/meet) my friend Sarah – and if I ¹¹ _____ (not/meet) Sarah, she ¹² _____ (not/introduce) me to her friend Jane. So Jane and I met because my taxi broke down that morning!

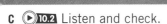

c ▶10.2 Listen and check.

2 VOCABULARY Expressions with *do*, *make* and *take*

a Match 1–6 with a–f to make sentences.

1 [c] They've offered me a job in Paris but I'm not sure if I want to take it or stay here. I have to make

2 [ ] If I had trained seriously over the past six months, I would have taken

3 [ ] I realise he isn't a very sociable person but please do

4 [ ] It's such a lovely day, so why don't we take

5 [ ] If we can rent the film on DVD, it doesn't make

6 [ ] His final exams are next month. If he did

a your best to persuade him to come to the party.

b advantage of the nice weather and go for a picnic by the river?

c a decision by the end of this week.

d sense for all five of us to go to the cinema to see it.

e badly he would have to repeat the whole year.

f part in last Sunday's marathon.

b Underline the correct words to complete the sentences.

1 Joe's a very outgoing and sociable boy so I'm sure he'll *do* / *make* / *take* new friends easily when he starts his new school.

2 You've *made* / *done* / *taken* a lot of progress with your English over the past six months. Well done!

3 We've been driving for over two hours now. Let's stop at the next service station and *make* / *do* / *take* a rest.

4 We're *doing* / *making* / *taking* some research into our family history. It's amazing what we've discovered.

5 I *did* / *made* / *took* a big mistake and called my father-in-law 'Tim' instead of 'Tom'. It was so embarrassing.

6 Who would *take* / *do* / *make* care of your grandmother if she were ill?

7 I've been *making* / *taking* / *doing* this maths homework all night and I still don't understand it.

3 PRONUNCIATION Strong and weak forms: *have*, *had* and *hadn't*

a ▶10.3 Listen to the pronunciation of *have* in these sentences. Is it strong (stressed) or weak (not stressed)? Write S (strong) or W (weak).

1 If I **hadn't** fallen over, I wouldn't **have** hurt my knee. [S]

2 We wouldn't **have** missed the bus if you **had** got up on time. [ ] [ ]

3 Julia would **have** passed her exams if she **had** worked harder. [ ] [ ]

4 If they **had** saved some money each week, they might **have** had enough to buy a car. [ ] [ ]

5 She would never **have** married him if she **had** known what a strange person he is. [ ] [ ]

10C Everyday English
You've got nothing to worry about

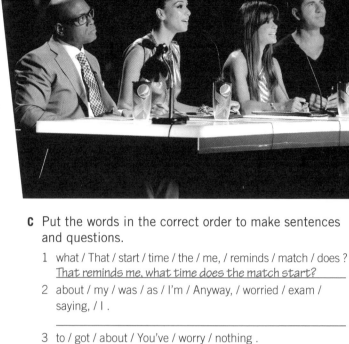

1 USEFUL LANGUAGE
Talking about possible problems and reassuring someone

a Complete the conversation with the words in the box.

> about   feeling   think   worried   nothing
> happen   it'll   ~~feel~~   definitely   what if

A How do you ¹___feel___ about the party tonight, then?

B Er, I'm ²_____ OK …

A Good. Is everything ready?

B Yes, but I'm ³_____ that not many people will come.

A You've got ⁴_____ to worry ⁵_____. You've invited lots of people.

B Yes, but ⁶_____ only a few people come?

A That's ⁷_____ not going to ⁸_____. Everyone I've spoken to says they're coming.

B Oh, good. You don't ⁹_____ we'll run out of food?

A No, I'm sure ¹⁰_____ be fine. You've made a lot of food and most people will probably bring something.

B Oh, OK, that's good.

b ▶10.4 Listen and check.

c Put the words in the correct order to make sentences and questions.

1 what / That / start / time / the / me, / reminds / match / does ?
That reminds me, what time does the match start?

2 about / my / was / as / I'm / Anyway, / worried / exam / saying, / I .
_____

3 to / got / about / You've / worry / nothing .
_____

4 *The X Factor* / music, / did / of / see / Speaking / night / last / you ?
_____

5 it / think / You / be / will / bit / boring / don't / a ?
_____

6 the / definitely / She's / like / going / ring / to .
_____

7 go / afraid / something / will / that / wrong / I'm .
_____

8 girlfriend / new / way, / have / By / you / the / his / met ?
_____

d ▶10.5 Listen and check.

2 PRONUNCIATION
Sounding sure and unsure

a ▶10.6 Listen to the exchanges. Does speaker B sound sure (falling intonation) or unsure (rising intonation)? Write S (sure) or U (unsure).

1 **A** How much will an engagement ring cost?
   B About £500. ☒ S

2 **A** How long has your sister known her boyfriend?
   B About four years. ☐

3 **A** What time does the film start?
   B At half past eight. ☐

4 **A** How often is there a train to York?
   B Every 45 minutes. ☐

5 **A** How fast was the car going when the accident happened?
   B About 100 kilometres an hour. ☐

6 **A** How much does it cost to fly to New York?
   B Around £600. ☐

Joe and Tom

bank have offered me the chance to go to
zil! Apparently, we're going to open a new
nch in Rio de Janeiro and my manager has
ed me if I'd like to go and work there. They
uld want me to stay for at least two years.
ink it would be an amazing opportunity to
abroad and to get some experience of
rking in a foreign country. It seems that they
uld provide me with free accommodation
pay for me to have Portuguese lessons.
at do you guys think? Would it be good for
career if I worked in Brazil for two years?
ase let me know what you think.
eak soon
an

Hi Brian

No wonder you sound so excited!
Everyone says Rio is a fantastic
place to live and that the Brazilians
are such friendly people. I think you
should definitely accept the offer.
I'm pretty sure you'd enjoy living
and working in Brazil and that you'd
make lots of new friends. Also, it
would look good on your CV if you
worked abroad for a couple of years.
And I'm sure it would be useful if you
learned another foreign language.
So, if I were you, I'd go for it.

Let me know what you decide to do.

Joe

P.S. I'd definitely come to visit you
for a holiday!

Hi Brian

I'm not sure what I think about the
opportunity you've been given to spend
two years in Brazil. I can see that it
would be exciting to live in Rio, but, if I
were you, I'd think about it very carefully
before making a decision.

I expect you'd have a great time in Rio
but you also need to think about your
career with the bank. You've worked
for your bank for over five years now so
maybe it would be better to apply for a
management job either with them or with
another bank in the UK? I'm not sure
experience of working in a bank in Brazil
would help when you come back to look
for a better job in London. I think you
should discuss with your manager what
kind of job your bank would give you if
you came back after two years.

Let me know if you want to meet up to
talk about it in more detail.

Best

Tom

1 READING

a Read the emails and tick (✓) the correct answer.

a ☐ Brian isn't sure if he should accept the job in Rio.
b ☐ Brian has already accepted the offer of a job in Brazil.
c ☐ Brian wants to leave his bank and get a new job.
d ☐ Brian has decided not to accept the job in Rio.

b Read the emails again. Are the sentences true or false?

1 Brian's bank want him to be the manager of their branch in Rio de Janeiro.
2 Brian wouldn't have to pay to rent a flat or a house in Rio.
3 Joe thinks that if Brian moves to Brazil he'll probably feel lonely.
4 Joe thinks it would be good for Brian's career to work in Brazil.
5 Tom doesn't think Brian would enjoy living in Rio.
6 Tom thinks working in Brazil for two years would definitely help Brian to get a better job in London.

2 WRITING SKILLS
Advising a course of action

a Complete the sentences with the words in the box.

should   better   definitely   would
I'd   pretty   expect   suggesting

1 If I were you, _____I'd_____ apply for that new job in Marketing.
2 I'm not sure you _____ enjoy working for that company.
3 It would _____ be good for your career.
4 I'm _____ sure you'd be a good manager.
5 Maybe it would be _____ to try and get another job in London?
6 I _____ you'd find that training course extremely interesting.
7 I think you _____ definitely discuss it with your manager.
8 I'm just _____ that you should think about it very carefully before you decide.

3 WRITING

a Read the email from Jane and write a reply. It can be positive and enthusiastic (in favour of her accepting the job) or more careful (advising her to consider going to university instead).

Hi

I've got some good news but I also need some advice.

I've just received my exam results and, fortunately, I passed all my subjects and even got a distinction in maths and IT. As a result, I've been offered a place at university to do a three-year degree in Business Studies. However, the problem is that my parents don't think I should go to university. Although my dad didn't go to university he's become a very successful businessman with a chain of small hotels around the country. Anyway, he wants me to start working as a trainee manager in one of these hotels. I worked there during the summer holidays last year as a receptionist and I really enjoyed it. So, I'm thinking of accepting his offer of a permanent job now instead of going to university. Apparently, I could become a hotel manager within five years.

Please let me know what you think.

Speak soon

Jane

61

UNIT 10
Reading and listening extension

1 READING

a Read the email. Complete the sentences with the names in the box. You need to use some names more than once.

Alex   Dean   Luis   Micky   Pilar   Robin   Stevo

1 _____Dean_____ wrote the email.
2 _____ received the email.
3 _____ and _____ are managers of local football teams.
4 _____ and _____ are football trainers.
5 _____ is the wife of one of the people in the email.

b Read the email again. Are the sentences true or false?

1 Dean respects Luis's knowledge of football.
2 Dean was mostly disappointed in the results of his team.
3 Dean thinks his team was most successful when they were attacking.
4 Dean has told his players that they are not allowed to have a rest.
5 Dean wants to reorganise his team.
6 Dean believes that most of his players try to avoid the ball during a game.
7 Dean agrees with Luis that the referee missed an important part of a recent game.
8 In general, Dean's email has been written in a formal style of English.

c Read the end of an email from your English friend, Emily. Write a positive and enthusiastic reply to Emily's email. Think about the following:

- how to begin your email
- how to advise her on the best course of action
- ways of encouraging Emily to become the manager.

Hi Luis!

How are things in Madrid these days? How are Pilar and the kids?

Thanks for your last email and for your excellent advice about goalkeepers. Your knowledge of football is just fantastic. Speaking of which, I need to ask your advice about something. So now that the team is taking a break from football for a couple of months, I thought that this would be a good time to think about next year.

Generally, I was quite proud of the players but I think we were beaten too many times. I'm convinced that we would have won more games if we had attacked better. The defence is strong but our attacking is just not so good. Although it's the summer holidays, I've already told the team that they cannot take it easy.

First of all, they're just not fit enough so they're all going to be doing more training. As I explained to them, 'If you're going to take part in this beautiful game, then you are going to have to work much harder. I don't want you to do your best – I want you to win, win, and then win again.' So from now on, they are going to do a good workout three times a week. Micky and Stevo (do you remember those guys?) are helping me do the training so I know that they'll have to work really hard.

I also want to have a go at changing the team. I don't think Alex or Robin should be in defence any more. I think both of them will be right for playing up front. I think they'd be good because they are the only two who aren't scared of the ball (you should see the rest of them!).

Anyway, that's what I thought after watching the videos of this year's games. For instance, that game we played against the All Stars in March. I think if we'd had those two at the front, then we would have won easily. Can I ask you to take a look at the video (the link's below)? Tell me what you think. That reminds me – I saw the video of your team's last game and I think you were right. If the referee had seen what number 7 had done to your goalkeeper, there would have been a penalty for sure.

Well, I won't write any more. As you know, there's no time to relax when you're the manager of the local primary school's seven-year-old girls' football team!

Best,

Dean

… so the local primary school is looking for a new manager for their girls' football team. The kids are seven years old, so they're quite little. I've been thinking about doing it.

I'm quite fit and I love football. Plus, I still haven't decided what to do after I finish university next year. Maybe if I do this, it will be good experience if I want to become a teacher later. It's voluntary, of course, and it's about 10 or 12 hours of my time every week.

What do you think? Does it sound worth doing?

Emily

2 LISTENING

a ▶10.7 Listen to a conversation between two students, Wendy and Phil, and tick (✓) the correct answers.

	Wendy	Phil
1 Who seems to be unhappy?	☐	☐
2 Who has had an interview recently?	☐	☐
3 Who wishes that they had got better marks at school?	☐	☐
4 Who describes a time when they felt very worried?	☐	☐
5 Who encourages the other?	☐	☐
6 Who needs some advice for a future interview?	☐	☐

b Listen to the conversation again. Tick (✓) the correct answers.

1 According to Wendy, how many people apply for each place at medical school?
   a ☐ 2
   b ☐ 10
   c ☐ 12

2 Phil reminds Wendy that she had excellent results in …
   a ☐ all her subjects.
   b ☐ more subjects than Phil.
   c ☐ most of her subjects.

3 When she describes her interview to Phil, what does Wendy compare herself to?
   a ☐ an animal
   b ☐ her mother
   c ☐ the Sahara desert

4 Phil is sure that the people who interviewed Wendy …
   a ☐ have all had a similar experience to Wendy.
   b ☐ must have understood how intelligent Wendy is.
   c ☐ were all experienced and professional people.

5 Wendy says that all doctors should be …
   a ☐ confident.
   b ☐ friendly.
   c ☐ patient.

6 Which of these things does Phil suggest might help Wendy improve?
   a ☐ taking up a sport
   b ☐ finding a job in a theatre
   c ☐ having a go at acting

c Choose a job from the box below. Write a conversation between two people. Person A has an interview for this job next week. Person B gives advice for the interview to Person A.

doctor   engineer   astronaut   politician   salesperson

Review and extension

1 GRAMMAR

Correct the sentences.

1 If I would speak French, I would apply for that job in Paris.
   If I spoke French, I would apply for that job in Paris.
2 If there wasn't an accident, we didn't miss our flight.
3 If I were you, I will wait until the shop has a sale to buy a jacket.
4 She didn't fail her exam if she studied harder.
5 If she would be nicer, she will make more friends.
6 We had caught the train on time if we left the house earlier.
7 I will buy a new car if I would have more money.
8 If it didn't rain yesterday, we would play tennis.

2 VOCABULARY

Correct the sentences.

1 The match finished 4 – 1 and Messi took three goals, including one penalty.
   The match finished 4 – 1 and Messi scored three goals, including one penalty.
2 I'm making some research into how children spend their pocket money.
3 In the final set Roger Federer won Rafael Nadal 6 – 2.
4 I'm terribly sorry, Madam, for doing a mistake with your bill.
5 My cousin's really good in languages – she speaks German, French and Russian.
6 Samantha's very worry about her exams.
7 He did a lot of money when he worked in the City of London, but now he's a teacher.
8 We've been working for two hours now, so let's do a short break and have a coffee.

3 WORDPOWER Easily confused words

Underline the correct words to complete the sentences.

1 Can you *bring* / *take* these flowers to your grandmother's house, please?
2 That man *stole* / *robbed* my mobile phone!
3 If we don't get to the station soon, we'll *lose* / *miss* our train.
4 In summer the sun *raises* / *rises* at 4.30 in the morning.
5 Can you *lend* / *borrow* me ten dollars, please?
6 He's *currently* / *actually* writing his third novel.

⟳ REVIEW YOUR PROGRESS

Look again at Review your progress on p.126 of the Student's Book. How well can you do these things now?
3 = very well   2 = well   1 = not so well

I CAN …

talk about new things I would like to do	☐
talk about imagined past events	☐
talk about possible problems and reassure someone	☐
write an email with advice.	☐

Vox pop video

Unit 1: Talk

🎥◀ What do you talk about when you're with your friends?

a Watch video 1a. Match 1–3 with a–c to make sentences.

1 ☐c☐ When she's with her friends, Jo usually talks about
2 ☐ ☐ When she's with her friends, Lauren usually talks about
3 ☐ ☐ When she's with her friends, Rachel usually talks about

a their boyfriends, husbands and holiday plans.
b their partners and other friends.
c going to museums, exhibitions and holidays.

🎥◀ What do you talk about when you're with your family?

b Watch video 1b. <u>Underline</u> the correct words to complete the sentences.

1 Jo *sometimes* / <u>*rarely*</u> / *always* discusses serious topics with her mother.
2 Rachel usually talks to her family about *friends* / *other family members* / *people in the news*.
3 Lauren has more interesting conversations with her *mother* / *brother* / *father*.

🎥◀ What language are you best at apart from your own?

c Watch video 1c and tick (✓) the correct answers.

1 Jo lived in Spain for _____.
   a ☐ 6 months
   b ☑ 12 months
   c ☐ 18 months

2 Now Jo's Spanish is _____ when she lived in Spain.
   a ☐ the same as
   b ☐ better than
   c ☐ not as good as

3 Rachel had the opportunity to practise her French when she was _____.
   a ☐ living in France
   b ☐ at school
   c ☐ at university

4 Rachel doesn't get the chance to speak _____ very often.
   a ☐ other languages
   b ☐ Spanish
   c ☐ French

5 Lauren speaks Spanish _____.
   a ☐ perfectly
   b ☐ badly
   c ☐ quite well

6 Lauren thinks it's hard to understand young people because they _____.
   a ☐ don't speak clearly
   b ☐ speak very quickly
   c ☐ have a strange accent

d Watch video 1c again. <u>Underline</u> the correct words to complete the sentences.

1 Jo wants more *Spanish lessons* / *Spanish friends* / <u>*trips to Spain*</u>.
2 Rachel *speaks several languages* / *only speaks English and French* / *speaks some German*.
3 Lauren doesn't know a lot of *formal Spanish* / *Spanish grammar* / *colloquial Spanish*.

Unit 2: Modern life

2a ◀ Which app do you use most?

a Watch video 2a. Match 1–4 with a–d to make sentences.

1 [c] James uses his favourite app to
2 [ ] Eugenia uses her favourite app to
3 [ ] Brian uses his favourite app to
4 [ ] Guy uses his favourite app to

a keep in touch with friends.
b avoid getting lost.
c send photos and messages.
d listen to music.

b Watch video 2a again and tick (✓) the correct answers.

1 James usually saves _____ photos.
   a [ ] all his
   b [ ] cool
   c [✓] funny

2 Eugenia thinks her app _____.
   a [ ] is difficult to use
   b [ ] is essential
   c [ ] is a lot of fun

3 Brian _____ his smartphone.
   a [ ] is obsessed with
   b [ ] plays games on
   c [ ] sometimes can't find

4 Guy uses his app to _____.
   a [ ] organise things
   b [ ] share videos with other people
   c [ ] stay in touch with his family

2b ◀ How many times have you been on social networking sites in the last week?

c Watch video 2b and tick (✓) the correct answers.

1 James mainly uses _____.
   a [ ] Instagram
   b [✓] Twitter
   c [ ] Facebook

2 Eugenia uses social networking sites to keep in touch with friends _____.
   a [ ] in her country
   b [ ] at university
   c [ ] in different countries

3 Brian goes on social networking sites _____ a day.
   a [ ] 7 – 13 times
   b [ ] 14 – 16 times
   c [ ] 17 times or more

4 Guy goes on social networking sites _____.
   a [ ] every day
   b [ ] every 2 days
   c [ ] 4 times a week

2c ◀ What do you like or dislike about social networking?

d Watch video 2c. Match 1–4 with a–d to make sentences.

1 [c] James likes
2 [ ] Eugenia talks about
3 [ ] Brian mentions
4 [ ] Guy discusses

a online bullying.
b the pressure to be friends with people online.
c free social media.
d living in another country.

e Watch video 2c again. Underline the correct words to complete the sentences.

1 James doesn't like the fact that *your friends* / *your family* / *companies* can have lots of information about you.
2 Eugenia likes the fact it's easy to keep in touch with her friends who live in *Cambridge* / *London* / *Chicago*.
3 Brian thinks that using text to communicate is *better than* / *very different from* / *not as good as* speaking to them in person.
4 Guy thinks that with social networking it's *fun* / *hard* / *easy* to organise things with friends.

Unit 3: Relationships

3a ◀ How did you first meet your best friend?

a Watch video 3a. Match 1–4 with a–d to make sentences.

1 [d] Heather met her best friend
2 [ ] Hannah met her best friend
3 [ ] Richard met his best friend
4 [ ] Maddy met her best friend

a when they were at nursery school together.
b when they were both working in Germany.
c through her family.
d when they worked for the same company.

3b ◀ How often do you see each other?

b Watch video 3b. Match 1–4 with a–d to make sentences.

1 [c] Heather and her best friend
2 [ ] Hannah and her best friend
3 [ ] Richard and his best friend
4 [ ] Maddy and her best friend

a see each other every day at school.
b talk on the phone together every two months.
c don't talk to each other on Skype.
d see each other every three weeks.

c Watch video 3b again. <u>Underline</u> the correct words to complete the sentences.

1 Heather and her best friend meet *every week / every couple of months / once a year.*

2 Hannah usually meets her best friend at *her house / school / a local café.*

3 Richard doesn't often see his best friend because *he doesn't have time / he lives a long way away / they don't have the same hobbies.*

4 Maddy and her best friend *are in the same class / live in the same house / play on the same team.*

3c ◀ What do you do together?

d Watch video 3c and tick (✓) the correct answers.

1 Heather enjoys _____ with her friend.
  a ☐ dancing
  b ☐ laughing
  c ✓ talking

2 Hannah enjoys _____ with her friend.
  a ☐ listening to music
  b ☐ staying at home
  c ☐ going to the park

3 Richard and his friend _____ together.
  a ☐ go to the park
  b ☐ go walking
  c ☐ laugh

4 Maddy and her friend _____ together.
  a ☐ dance a lot
  b ☐ laugh a lot
  c ☐ listen to music

e Watch video 3c again. Match 1–4 with a–d to make sentences.

1 ☐a Heather and her best friend
2 ☐ Hannah and her best friend
3 ☐ Richard and his best friend
4 ☐ Maddy and her best friend

a like to have lunch together.
b are like family.
c go walking around together.
d like to complain about modern life.

Unit 4: Personality

4a ◀ Can you tell me about something you're very good at?

a Watch video 4a. Match 1–4 with a–d to make sentences.

1 ☐c Who is very good at martial arts?
2 ☐ Who can draw very well?
3 ☐ Who has stopped doing a sport because of an injury?
4 ☐ Who doesn't usually get lost when visiting a new place?

a Ollie
b Margaret
c Chris
d John

b Watch video 4a again and tick (✓) the correct answers.

1 Ollie stopped rowing because _____.
  a ☐ he lost lots of competitions
  b ✓ he had an injury
  c ☐ his friends stopped doing it

2 Margaret _____ takes a map with her when she goes to a new place.
  a ☐ always
  b ☐ hardly ever
  c ☐ usually

3 Chris has a hobby from _____.
  a ☐ China
  b ☐ Russia
  c ☐ the USA

4 When he was younger, John was good at _____.
  a ☐ acting
  b ☐ playing an instrument
  c ☐ sports

4b ◀ **Can you tell me about something you're not very good at?**

c Watch video 4b. <u>Underline</u> the correct words to complete the sentences.

1 Ollie isn't very good at *maths* / <u>*French*</u> / *sport*.
2 Margaret thinks speaking *in meetings* / *in public* / *to strangers* is difficult.
3 Chris isn't very good at *sport* / *spelling* / *languages*.
4 John doesn't think enough about what he *eats* / *says* / *wears*.

4c ◀ **What do you think is the most important skill to have?**

d Watch video 4c. Match 1–4 with a–d to make sentences.

1 [c] Ollie thinks that it's important to be able to
2 [ ] Margaret thinks that it's important to be able to
3 [ ] Chris thinks that it's important to be able to
4 [ ] John thinks that it's important to be able to

a communicate effectively.
b listen to other people.
c interact with other people.
d hold a good conversation.

Unit 5: The natural world

5a ◀ **Is pollution a problem where you live?**

a Watch video 5a. <u>Underline</u> the correct words to complete the sentences.

1 Where Anna lives the *sea* / <u>*river*</u> / *streets* used to be very polluted.
2 Where Anna lives people leave a lot of litter *in the park* / *on the beach* / *in the street*.
3 Where Matt lives the *land* / *river* / *air* is quite polluted.
4 Martina thinks that *the rivers are* / *the air is* / *the roads are* cleaner in the countryside.
5 Martina says that in London the pollution is mainly caused by *cars and lorries* / *people* / *aeroplanes*.
6 Lauren says that there *is a lot of* / *isn't very much* / *isn't any* pollution in Cambridge.

b Watch video 5a again and tick (✓) the correct answers.

1 Anna mentions _____ in her local area.
   a [ ] the trees and plants
   b [ ] the weather
   c [✓] the wildlife
2 Matt mentions local _____.
   a [ ] farmers
   b [ ] politicians
   c [ ] shops

3 Martina says the road near her house makes her home _____.
   a [ ] dangerous
   b [ ] dirty
   c [ ] noisy
4 Lauren says that there are a lot of _____ in Cambridge.
   a [ ] bikes
   b [ ] cars
   c [ ] trains

5b ◀ **What can people do to help the environment?**

c Watch video 5b. Match 1–4 with a–d to make sentences.

1 [c] Anna thinks that
2 [ ] Matt thinks that
3 [ ] Martina thinks that
4 [ ] Lauren thinks that

a people shouldn't travel short distances by plane.
b more people should cycle to work.
c more children should walk to school.
d people should try and recycle their old clothes.

d Watch video 5b again. <u>Underline</u> the correct words to complete the sentences.

1 Anna says her husband should <u>*be more organised*</u> / *cycle more often* / *recycle more*.
2 Matt does not mention *recycling* / *travelling by plane* / *saving water*.
3 Martina feels *bad about* / *proud of* / *satisfied with* what she does to help the environment.
4 Lauren mentions recycling *glass* / *metals* / *paper*.

5c◀ How do you think the climate will change in the next hundred years?

e Watch video 5c. Match 1–4 with a–d to make sentences.

1. [c] Anna thinks that
2. [ ] Matt thinks that
3. [ ] Martina thinks that
4. [ ] Lauren thinks that

a in the UK the weather will never be extremely hot.
b average temperatures in the UK will be higher.
c our summers will be warmer and our winters will be cooler.
d sea levels will be higher and it will be warmer.

Unit 6: Different cultures

6a◀ Do you like visiting foreign countries?

a Watch video 6a. Underline the correct words to complete the sentences.

1. Martina likes going to foreign countries because the *weather* / *culture* / *coffee* is different.
2. Maibritt thinks it's *boring* / *interesting* / *exciting* to visit other countries.
3. Matt thinks it's *exciting* / *interesting* / *expensive* to travel to different parts of the world.
4. Anna thinks it's interesting to see what the *houses look like* / *public transport looks like* / *shops look like*.

b Watch video 6a again. Match 1–4 with a–d to make sentences.

1. [b] Martina talks about
2. [ ] Maibritt talks about
3. [ ] Matt talks about
4. [ ] Anna talks about

a the architecture in other countries.
b the fruit in other countries.
c the trains in other countries.
d the weather in other countries.

6b◀ Have you ever experienced culture shock?

c Watch video 6b. Match 1–8 with a–h to make sentences.

1. [c] Martina worked as a volunteer in
2. [ ] Martina was surprised
3. [ ] Maibritt spent two years in
4. [ ] Maibritt was surprised
5. [ ] Matt taught English in
6. [ ] Matt was surprised
7. [ ] Anna had a job as a teaching assistant in
8. [ ] Anna was surprised

a Japan.
b by how different it was from Great Britain.
c Russia.
d by the role of women.
e that people didn't use 'small talk'.
f Germany.
g by how people spoke to each other.
h Italy.

d Watch video 6b again and tick (✓) the correct answers.

1. Martina spent _____ in Russia.
   a [ ] a month
   b [✓] half a year
   c [ ] six years
2. Maibritt mentions that she had problems with _____ abroad.
   a [ ] eating new things
   b [ ] finding her way around
   c [ ] working
3. Matt felt _____ during his first weeks in Japan.
   a [ ] angry
   b [ ] excited
   c [ ] scared
4. Anna had problems getting to know her colleagues in Germany because _____.
   a [ ] she didn't speak the language
   b [ ] she was extremely shy around new people
   c [ ] there was an age difference between her and them

6c◀ What advice would you give someone visiting this country for the first time?

e Watch video 6c. Match 1–4 with a–d to make sentences.

1. [c] Martina says that
2. [ ] Maibritt says that
3. [ ] Matt says that
4. [ ] Anna says that

a tourists should try English food and go to a football match.
b it can rain at any time in the UK.
c tourists should explore the British countryside.
d the weather in the UK changes all the time.

Unit 7: House and home

7a ◀ **Did you grow up in a big city or a small town?**

a Watch video 7a. <u>Underline</u> the correct words to complete the sentences.

1 Deborah liked the *parks* / <u>*people*</u> / *weather* in Manchester.
2 Tony *lives* / *would like to live* / *doesn't live* in the village where he was born.
3 Andrew liked living in Cardiff because of the *culture* / *weather* / *people*.
4 Arian liked Cambridge because there were lots of *friendly people* / *parks for children* / *good schools*.

b Watch video 7a again and tick (✓) the correct answers.

1 Deborah complains about the _____ in Manchester.
   a ☐ prices
   b ☐ public transport
   c ✓ weather
2 Tony is _____ the place where he lives.
   a ☐ fed up with
   b ☐ frustrated with
   c ☐ happy with
3 Andrew describes Cardiff as good for _____.
   a ☐ shopping
   b ☐ outdoor activities
   c ☐ tourism
4 Arian thinks that Cambridge is _____.
   a ☐ enormous
   b ☐ not large
   c ☐ a typical city

7b ◀ **What are the advantages of living in a big city?**

c Watch video 7b. Match 1–4 with a–d to make sentences.

1 ☐ *c* Deborah thinks that in a big city
2 ☐ Margaret thinks that in a big city
3 ☐ Andrew thinks that in a big city
4 ☐ Arian thinks that in a big city

a there are lots of people to meet.
b there are always plenty of interesting things to do.
c it's easy to see a film or an exhibition.
d everything you need is near to where you live.

7c ◀ **What are the disadvantages of living in a big city?**

d Watch video 7c and tick (✓) the correct answers.

1 Deborah _____ living in a big city.
   a ☐ loves
   b ☐ doesn't enjoy
   c ✓ doesn't mind
2 Tony thinks that if you live in a big city, you might miss _____ .
   a ☐ your friends
   b ☐ the countryside
   c ☐ your village
3 Andrew thinks that cities are _____ than villages.
   a ☐ cleaner
   b ☐ more polluted
   c ☐ friendlier
4 Arian says that people _____ in a big city.
   a ☐ don't know all their neighbours
   b ☐ don't have many friends
   c ☐ are always very busy

Unit 8: Information

🎥 8a◀ When did you last read a newspaper?

a Watch video 8a and tick (✓) the correct answers.

1 Alyssia read the *i* newspaper because it _____.
- a ☐ was the only one on sale
- b ☐ was given to her free
- c ✓ wasn't expensive

2 Tom _____ a copy of the *Metro* newspaper.
- a ☐ bought
- b ☐ was given
- c ☐ couldn't find

3 Lottie _____ newspapers.
- a ☐ doesn't usually buy
- b ☐ doesn't like reading
- c ☐ can't afford to buy

4 Tim read the *Independent* newspaper _____.
- a ☐ last weekend
- b ☐ yesterday
- c ☐ today

5 Elizabeth read *The Times* because _____.
- a ☐ it's her favourite newspaper
- b ☐ her father left it
- c ☐ it was cheap to buy

b Watch video 8a again. Underline the correct words to complete the sentences.

1 Alyssia says she last read a newspaper *the day before yesterday* / *yesterday* / *that morning*.
2 Tom read the newspaper *at home* / *in a café* / *on the train*.
3 Lottie looks at the papers when she's *at home* / *shopping* / *waiting for the bus*.
4 Tim read the *Guardian* / the *Independent* / the *Metro*.
5 Elizabeth *always* / *occasionally* / *usually* reads *The Times*.

🎥 8b◀ Where do you get most of your news from?

c Watch video 8b. Match 1–5 with a–e to make sentences.

1 ☐c☐ Alyssia gets her news
2 ☐ Tom sometimes reads the news
3 ☐ Lottie gets her news
4 ☐ Tim normally gets his news
5 ☐ Elizabeth reads about the week's news

a from BBC1.
b on the Internet.
c from television news channels.
d in a magazine.
e from newspapers.

🎥 8c◀ What kinds of news are you most interested in?

d Watch video 8c. Underline the correct words to complete the sentences.

1 Alyssia is most interested in *entertainment news* / *local news* / *world affairs*.
2 Tom likes *sports* / *entertainment* / *business* news.
3 Lottie is most interested in *celebrity* / *entertainment* / *international* news.
4 Tim likes *local* / *business* / *celebrity* news.
5 Elizabeth is interested in news about *fashion* / *world affairs* / *people*.

e Watch video 8c again and tick (✓) the correct answers.

1 Alyssia says she is interested in _____ news.
- a ☐ culture
- b ✓ politics
- c ☐ technology

2 Tom is studying _____.
- a ☐ economics
- b ☐ film studies
- c ☐ history of art

3 Lottie thinks that reading gossip about stars is _____.
- a ☐ boring
- b ☐ fun
- c ☐ terrific

4 Tim is originally from _____.
- a ☐ Canada
- b ☐ Ireland
- c ☐ the USA

5 Elizabeth isn't interested in news about _____.
- a ☐ entertainment
- b ☐ finance
- c ☐ other cultures

Unit 9: Entertainment

🎥 9a◀ How much TV do you watch?

a Watch video 9a and tick (✓) the correct answers.

1 Colin watches _____ a day.
- a ✓ 1 hour
- b ☐ 2 hours
- c ☐ 3 hours

2 Jessie watches _____ a day.
- a ☐ half an hour
- b ☐ 1 hour
- c ☐ 2 hours

3 Caroline watches _____.
- a ☐ 30 minutes a day
- b ☐ 1 hour a day
- c ☐ only at weekends

4 Dave _____ watches TV.
- a ☐ often
- b ☐ rarely
- c ☐ never

5 Gary watches _____.
- a ☐ 1 hour a day
- b ☐ 1 hour a week
- c ☐ 1 hour a month

9b ◀ What kind of TV programmes do you like?

b Watch video 9b. Match 1–4 with a–d to make sentences.

1 [c] Colin likes watching
2 ☐ Jessie likes watching
3 ☐ Caroline likes watching
4 ☐ Dave likes watching

a sports programmes.
b reality TV programmes.
c documentaries.
d crime dramas.

9c ◀ Can you recommend a great film?

c Watch video 9c. Underline the correct words to complete the sentences.

1 The film Colin recommends is a *comedy* / *drama* / *horror* film.
2 Jessie saw a great film *last week* / *last month* / *several years ago*.
3 The film Caroline recommends is a good film for *children* / *adults* / *the whole family*.
4 When you watch Dave's film, you will feel *happy* / *excited* / *sad*.

d Watch video 9c again. Match 1–4 with a–d to make sentences.

1 [b] Colin recommends his film because
2 ☐ Jessie recommends her film because
3 ☐ Caroline recommends her film because
4 ☐ Dave recommends his film because

a it gives people hope.
b it stars great actors.
c it's very funny.
d it has an interesting central idea.

Unit 10: Opportunities

10a ◀ How often do you play sport?

a Watch video 10a and tick (✓) the correct answers.

1 Chloe plays sport _____.
   a ☐ once a week
   b ✓ several times a week
   c ☐ once a month

2 Alwyn plays golf _____.
   a ☐ once a week
   b ☐ every day
   c ☐ at least once a month

3 Steph goes skiing _____.
   a ☐ once a year
   b ☐ twice a year
   c ☐ several times a year

4 Trevis _____ plays sport.
   a ☐ often
   b ☐ sometimes
   c ☐ never

5 Claire goes to the gym _____.
   a ☐ every day
   b ☐ twice a week
   c ☐ once a week

10b ◀ Would you like to run a marathon?

b Watch video 10b. Match 1–5 with a–e to make sentences.

1 [c] Chloe wouldn't like to run a marathon because
2 ☐ Alwyn wouldn't like to run a marathon because
3 ☐ Steph wouldn't like to run a marathon because
4 ☐ Trevis wouldn't like to run a marathon because
5 ☐ Claire wouldn't like to run a marathon because

a it would be too tiring.
b she finds it uncomfortable to run.
c she's afraid of pain.
d it's not a good idea for an old person.
e she hasn't got enough energy.

c Watch video 10b again. Underline the correct words to complete the sentences.

1 Chloe would *never run a marathon* / *run a full marathon* / *run a half-marathon*.
2 Alwyn says his *best friend* / *daughter* / *wife* has run a marathon.
3 Steph *criticises* / *respects* / *wants to be like* people who run marathons.
4 Trevis *is not interested in* / *has stopped* / *got injured* running marathons.
5 Claire only runs *for the bus* / *when she's on holiday* / *in the gym*.

10c ◀ If you could try one new sport, what would it be?

d Watch video 10c. Match 1–5 with a–e to make sentences.

1 [e] If Chloe had a lot of money,
2 ☐ If Alwyn were fit enough,
3 ☐ Steph likes doing crazy things, so
4 ☐ If Trevis could try a new sport,
5 ☐ If Claire could try a new sport,

a she would choose beach volleyball.
b she would try base-jumping.
c she would choose paddle boarding.
d he would try snowboarding.
e she would try paraskiing.

Audioscripts

Unit 1

▶ 1.1

1 **A** Well, if you ask me, Tanya Davies would be the best person for the job.
   B Actually, I don't agree. As far as I'm concerned, Luke Adams would be better.
2 **A** Well, I guess you could take the shoes back to the shop.
   B I'm not so sure about that. I've already worn them.
3 **A** I think it's going to be difficult to make enough money to survive.
   B Yes, I see where you're coming from. Maybe we should find a cheaper office?
4 **A** Well, in my opinion, Italian is easier than French.
   B I know what you mean. I think it's easier to pronounce.

▶ 1.2

1 **A** It seems to me that their coffee is better than ours.
   B Yes, I know exactly what you mean. It's really smooth, isn't it?
2 **A** As far as I'm concerned, I think it makes sense to take the train to Paris.
   B I'm not so sure about that. It takes nearly three hours.
3 **A** I think Germany will probably win the football World Cup.
   B Yes, I think that's right. They've got the best team.
4 **A** Well, in my opinion, we need to find another business partner in Spain.
   B Yes, I see where you're coming from. Maybe a company based in Madrid this time?

▶ 1.3

1 **A** Guess what, Tony? I've just read about this girl, and she's only ten but she's fluent in several different languages.
   B That's fantastic. I can only speak one language – English.
2 **A** Hi, Linda. Are you learning Russian?
   B I'm trying to! But this book's useless! It teaches you how to say 'my uncle's black trousers' but not how to say 'hello'!

▶ 1.4

JOE So, Bridget, are you going to tell me about your website? Are you working on it at the moment?
BRIDGET Yes, it's almost ready, but it isn't finished just yet.
J And who's it for?
B Well, you remember what I'm studying, don't you?
J Yes, uh, well. You're studying French or Spanish or something, aren't you?
B Well, sort of. I'm in the Latin American studies department so yes I learn Spanish but I also study history, culture, politics – all that kind of thing.
J Oh right. So the website is for the Latin American studies students?
B Yes, but not just for them. It's also for students of Spanish and for students from the World History department too. They're all going to use it. And all the information on it has to be in Spanish as well as English so that I can keep in touch with all the students I met at UNAM.
J UNAM?
B Oh, that's the name of the university in Mexico where I was studying.
J Oh, I see. So, are you writing everything in Spanish as well as English?
B Yes, I'm completely exhausted!
J I'm not surprised! That sounds like an absolutely enormous job!
B Well, I'm not doing everything on my own. There's a Colombian girl, Monica, she's helping me to check my grammar and spelling and stuff.
J Oh, OK. So what can I do to help?
B Well, I'm not very good at web design so would you have any time to look at it for me? I need someone to check that everything on the website is working properly.
J Well, I'm a little busy …
B You have to help me, Joe! You're my only hope!
J OK, OK. I'll help you!
B Wonderful! So, I've chosen the main photo for the website. But I thought maybe I could ask your opinion?
J Sure, let's have a look.
B Great. It's here on my iPad.
J Wow! This is great! Where's this place?
B It's called Chichen Itza.
J Is that the name of the pyramid in the middle of the photo?
B No, Chichen Itza's the name of the ancient city. The pyramid … I can't remember what the name of the pyramid is.
J Well anyway, it's a great photo for your website. It's got history, and culture and it just looks really cool.
B Great! So, when can you help me with the design of the website? Do you have any time …

Unit 2

▶ 2.1

1 I applied for lots of jobs.
2 We've worked very hard today.
3 I've learnt a lot in this job.
4 They offered me more money.
5 You've had a fantastic career at the BBC.

▶ 2.2

1 Could you ask your brother to help you?
2 Oh, really? That's a shame.
3 How about taking it back to the shop where you bought it?
4 I'm really glad to hear that.
5 Why don't you try talking to your boss about it?
6 Let's take it to the garage.
7 Oh dear. How annoying!
8 Shall we ask his girlfriend what kind of music he likes?

▶ 2.3

A I've lost my phone!
B Oh, no. How awful!
A I've been looking for it everywhere. I'm sure I had it when I got home.
B What about checking in your bag?
A OK … No, it isn't in there …
B ok, so it isn't in your bag. Have you tried phoning your number from another phone?
A That's a great idea. I'll give it a try. Can I borrow your phone for a minute?
B Yes, sure. Here you are.
A Oh, listen – it's ringing! It's behind that cushion on the sofa!
B That's brilliant! I'm so pleased!

▶ 2.4

1 Barbara's just bought a new car and it won't start!
2 My boss has been criticising my work recently.
3 My neighbours had a party last night so I didn't sleep very well.
4 My computer's been running very slowly since I installed that new program.

▶ 2.5

DIANE So, Carlos, how was your journey this morning? Did you drive or …?
CARLOS Oh, it was fine thank you. I came by train from London.
D I see. Right, well, let's start, shall we? To begin with I'll ask you a few questions about your CV and your education, your work experience and so on and then Steven is going to talk to you about the job. OK? Any questions so far?
C No, no, everything is fine so far, thank you.
D Great! OK, so can you tell me a little bit about yourself?
C Yes, of course. So, I'm 23 years old and I have just recently completed a university course in Computer Science. And that was in London, where I've been living for the last three, in fact, almost four years now. Before coming to England I was at school in Spain.
D Ah yes, that's right, I see from your CV that you went to high school in Madrid.
C Yes. Although, I was actually born in San Francisco. But when I was 14 I moved to Spain to live with my grandparents, who are from Madrid.
D Ah, so you are a Spanish speaker, then?
C Yes. And as well as English and Spanish I also speak German. That's because of my father. He's an engineer from Düsseldorf.
D I see. That's very impressive. As you may already know, this company has offices in several different European countries so we're keen to find people who can speak at least one other language as well as English.
C Well, that's good. I'd like the chance to use my languages.
D OK, now, in your opinion, why should this organisation choose you for this job?
C That's a very good question. Well, first of all I'm a people person. I'm very friendly and so I have a real ability to work in a team. Specialist knowledge is important, but you also need to be able to explain ideas simply and clearly. And that's something that I think I've learned in the job I do now. And I think it's been a good experience for this job.
D And why's that, may I ask? We don't really meet any customers in this job.
C True. But I soon learned that the best way to sell a phone wasn't to talk about all the technical things – it was to show people the apps! I discovered that I could sell more phones if I used clear and simple language to explain how to use them. So for almost three years now, I've been staying up to date on all the most popular apps and selling more phones than anyone else.
D Very interesting. OK, now, …

Unit 3

▶ 3.1

1 Mark and Tania got to know each other when they worked in Spain.
2 They've got lots of shared interests.
3 He gets on very well with his aunt.
4 I'm not very good at keeping in touch with old friends.
5 What does she have in common with her American cousin?

▶ 3.2

1 The best thing is that my new flat is air conditioned.
2 Anyway, we still hadn't found a hotel for my grandparents.
3 In the end, we bought him a computer game.
4 It turned out that he had never played golf in his life.
5 You'll never guess what Sarah said to David.
6 The funny thing was that he didn't know she was joking.
7 You won't believe what he bought her for her birthday. A snake!
8 To make matters worse, the water was too cold to have a shower.

▶ 3.3

1 You'll never guess what happened at the party.
2 The best thing is that it's got a swimming pool.
3 Anyway, we still had to find a present for Maggie.
4 To make matters worse, it started raining heavily.

5 You won't believe what I did on Saturday.
6 The funny thing was that she didn't realise what had happened.
7 In the end, he agreed to drive us to the station.
8 It turned out that she had lost her train ticket.

▶ **3.4**

1 But, anyway, the train was still at the station and we got on just as the doors were closing.
2 In the end, we went to a little restaurant near the station, where we had a lovely meal.
3 To make matters worse, the waiter dropped the bottle of wine and it ruined my new white dress.
4 On top of that, when she eventually got to the airport they told her that her flight was nearly two hours late.
5 Anyway, in the end I found a lovely flat in the centre, and the best thing is that it's only eight hundred euros a month!

▶ **3.5**

ROSIE Hi there! Hi, my name's Rosie Cameron and I'm a student here at the university. Do you have a few minutes?

BEN Oh, uh, sure. What do you need?

R Well, I'm doing a questionnaire on family and friendship, so would it be OK to ask you some questions?

B Sure, no problem.

R Great! Thank you so much! OK, so can you tell me your name and what you do?

B Sure. My name's Ben. Ben Boole. And I'm a second-year politics student.

R Well, hello Ben! Oh I've said that already, haven't I? OK, so you're male – obviously – and your age group is 18 to 24?

B A bit older, actually. I'm 28. So you need to tick the 25 to 32 box.

R Twenty-eight. Great, thanks. OK, so first question. Are you in a relationship?

B No, I'm single at the moment.

R No way!

B What?

R Nothing! Sorry – not married, no girlfriend – OK, next question! When you meet people for the first time, do you find it easy to make friends with them?

B Yes, I think so. I'm not shy. In fact, I think I'm generally quite confident.

R OK, and how would you describe your childhood?

B Really happy. Um, I grew up in quite a big family: there was my mum and dad, of course, but I've also got five older sisters.

R Wow, so you're the youngest of six children, then?

B Yeah, that's right. But I also lived with two of my grandparents – my mum's mum and dad.

R So there were three generations and ten people living in the same house, then? Wow.

B Yes. Basically, I was brought up in a house full of women. My grandmother, my mum, and my elder sisters. I think that's why I'm quite confident now. Because I had so much support when I was growing up, I mean.

R How cool! OK, do you keep in touch with friends you made at school?

B Yes, I've got a friend called 'Zippy'. Actually, his real name's Sipho, Sipho Zulu. His dad's from Zimbabwe. But everyone calls him Zippy.

R And did you get on with Zippy straight away?

B No! Actually, that was the funny thing. Before we met, I'd been the best football player in the whole school.

R Oh, I'm sure you were.

B Sorry?

R Nothing!

B Uh, so anyway Zippy was such a good player that I really hated him at first.

R So how did you become friends?

B Well, we eventually discovered that we had lots of things in common. He's also the youngest child in a big family and he also only has older sisters. And we definitely share the same sense of humour.

R How important is a sense of humour in friendship?

B Oh, really important! I mean …

Unit 4

▶ **4.1**

1 You don't smoke any more, do you?
2 It's a lovely day today, isn't it?
3 Tom isn't going to ask her to marry him, is he?
4 You haven't been waiting long for me, have you?
5 She'd already bought him a present, hadn't she?
6 They'll phone us when they get to the airport, won't they?
7 The twins both got good grades in their exams, didn't they?
8 Andrew speaks five languages fluently, doesn't he?
9 You don't want any rice, Jim, do you?

▶ **4.2**

1 **A** I wondered if you could do me a favour?
 B Sure, how can I help you?
 A Do you think you could cut the grass in my garden for me?
 B Yes, of course. No problem.
2 **A** I've got a lot of things to get ready for the party tomorrow night.
 B Is there something I can do?
 A Yes, there is, actually. Can you give me a hand with the shopping?
 B Yes, that's fine. Could I ask you a favour in return?
 A Go ahead!
 B Could you lend me your black trousers for tomorrow?
 A No problem. I'll just get them for you.
3 **A** Could I ask you a favour, Ben?
 B Of course, what do you need?
 A Could you help me move my desk into the other office?
 B Actually, I've got a bad back. Can you ask someone else?

▶ **4.3**

1 You've been to Cairo before, haven't you?
2 Jack's really good at tennis, isn't he?
3 They've got four children, haven't they?
4 This is the best beach in Thailand, isn't it?
5 You're glad you left London, aren't you?
6 You didn't go to Canada last year, did you?

▶ **4.4**

Thank you, thank you. OK! So my talk tonight is called 'Psychology in Advertising', but I'm going to start with a little story.

In the 18th century, Germany was divided into lots of different countries and one of these was called Prussia, and the king there was called Frederick the Second. Now this particular king was a really very talented man. In fact, he was so brilliant that he is still known as Frederick the Great.

OK, so at that time, the 1770s, hardly anyone in Prussia ate potatoes, because the main meal for almost everyone was bread. But there was a problem with bread: in those days, sometimes the wheat didn't grow very well, or it grew but then it died before people could make bread from it. And every time that happened, people, especially poor people, would have nothing to eat.

So when Frederick heard about the potato, he thought 'A-ha! Perfect! If the people can grow these potatoes as well as bread, then no one will ever be hungry again!'

Frederick was so satisfied with this idea that he immediately ordered everyone in the country to start growing potatoes. But to his surprise, they refused. They simply would not touch these potatoes. The people of Kolberg sent Frederick a letter, telling him that potatoes were so disgusting that even their animals couldn't eat them.

Now Frederick was a very intelligent man, and although there were no psychologists in 1774, he certainly had a talent for understanding the psychology of his people. So he soon came up with a very interesting plan.

First, he planted potatoes in a big field, which he called the 'Royal Potato Garden'. Next, because it was not just any potato garden, but the Royal Potato Garden, he sent soldiers to guard it.

As soon as people saw the garden and the soldiers, they started asking each other 'What could be in that field that is worth so much?' And of course, as soon as they found out that the field was full of potatoes, they all wanted some. It was not long afterwards that people started going to the field at night to steal potatoes. Frederick, of course, had expected this to happen. In fact, he had even given secret instructions to his soldiers to pretend that they had not seen the potato thieves and actually let them steal the potatoes, because that was what Frederick had wanted to happen.

There is an important lesson here for people about psychology in advertising.

When Frederick told people they would never be hungry again if they ate potatoes – they were not interested. When Frederick ordered them to grow potatoes – they refused. But when people believed that they were not allowed to eat potatoes, and that they were only eaten by kings and queens, then they immediately wanted to have them. And that's good psychology.

Unit 5

▶ **5.1**

/eɪ/: save, danger, education, nature
/ɑː/: plant, park, after, branch
/æ/: charity, animal, mammal, dam
/ə/: local, abroad, gorilla, along

▶ **5.2**

1 If they offer me the job, I'm going to move to London.
2 We'll phone you when our plane lands at Glasgow Airport.
3 If we don't stop hunting tigers, they'll be extinct in 20 years' time.
4 When the weather gets too cold, the birds fly south.
5 My dad will buy me a new laptop if I help him paint the house.
6 If you feel hungry later, have a banana or an apple.
7 I'll be there at 11 o'clock unless there's a problem with the train.
8 Unless the bus comes soon, I'm going to take a taxi.

▶ **5.3**

1 Alice doesn't enjoy her current job because she often has to work until 8 pm.
2 There are lots of things I can offer this company, like my talent for creating attractive websites and my experience of management.
3 It took me over an hour to get to work this morning due to a serious accident on the motorway.
4 **A** There are some things I don't like about my job.
 B Such as?
 A Well, for instance, I don't like having to drive 50 km to work every day.
5 Tom didn't get on with his new boss so he decided to apply for a job with another company.
6 Since there weren't any meeting rooms free at 11 o'clock, they had to hold the meeting in his office.
7 I had to stay late at work yesterday. As a result, I didn't get home until nine o'clock.
8 My train arrived 45 minutes late this morning because of the bad weather in Scotland.

▶ **5.4**

1 **A** So how old is your father now?
 B Let me see. I think he'll be 62 in June.
2 **A** So what skills can you bring to this job?
 B Well, to begin with, I've got excellent computer skills.
3 **A** So why do you want to leave your current job?
 B That's a good question. The main reason is that I need a new challenge.
4 **A** What time does their plane arrive at Heathrow Airport?
 B Just a second. I'll check on their website.

▶ **5.5**

1 bore
2 pear
3 cap
4 bloom
5 cup

▶ **5.6**

Thank you, thank you. So, I'd like to begin today with something that the British writer, Theodore Dalrymple, once said.

Walking through the streets of the city where he lives, he starts to notice piles of rubbish everywhere he looks. And not just any rubbish, but the rubbish left behind by people who have bought food. And not just any food, but fast food, junk food.

Seeing all this, he asks himself: What did it mean? All this litter? At the very least, it suggested that an Englishman's street is his dining room … as well as his dustbin.

I wanted to share this with you because – well, partly because it is true, of course. Anyone who lives or has lived in a modern British city will recognise that description. But I have another reason for sharing that story with you and that is that I want you to understand that pollution is not just something that happens to the natural environment or even to the wildlife that lives in it. It happens here, where we live. As I will explain during this talk, we cannot expect to improve the natural world if we do not first improve the condition of our own streets and cities. How can we expect to protect the environment from pollution when our own streets are full of rubbish?

In other words, we need to clean our own streets before we can even dream about preventing pollution in the rainforests of the Amazon, or the seas and oceans. And it is important to understand that the damage that we do to the world is not just 'out there'. It is here, and with us, all of the time. And we also need to remember that when we do damage to our environment we are actually doing damage to ourselves.

So my talk today is called 'Save yourself!' and my message is simple: we have to help ourselves before we can hope to help wildlife or the environment.

My talk is going to be in three parts. First of all, I will say some more about the problem of rubbish in the local areas where we live. It is now possible for us to manage our rubbish in a way that is environmentally friendly – but we don't. So in this part of my talk, I'm going to be asking 'Why not? Why, when it is possible to be more environmentally friendly, do most people seem not to care?'.

Next, I will discuss the problem of people. There are currently seven billion of us in the world and that is almost twice the number of people living in the world 50 years ago. For this reason, I will suggest that we need to change people's minds and I will also describe some ways of doing this. Ways that I think, I hope, will be successful in the future.

Finally, I will show how protecting your local area is the first step to protecting the planet for future generations of children.

Unit 6

▶ **6.1**

PAUL I've got my English exam tomorrow morning.
MUM Oh, really? So what time do you have to be at school?
P Well, the exam starts at 9 o'clock, so I mustn't be late.
M I think you ought to leave earlier than normal, in case there's a lot of traffic.
P Yes, that's a good idea.
M And what are you going to do after the exam?
P Well, I don't have to stay at school in the afternoon, so I can come home for lunch.
M Fine, just two more things. It says on this information sheet that students must show their identity cards to the examiner before the exam.
P Don't worry. I always take my ID card with me to school.
M It also says you can't use a dictionary during the exam, so don't take one with you.
P Yes, I know. I'll leave it at home.
M OK, good. By the way, it's 10 o'clock. You shouldn't go to bed late tonight.
P No, you're right. I'll go up now.
M OK, good night. And good luck for tomorrow!

▶ **6.2**

1 swimming pool
2 rush hour
3 washing machine
4 cycle lane
5 lunchtime
6 cash machine

▶ **6.3**

1 My meal wasn't nearly as nice as I expected.
2 This is by far the most luxurious hotel I've ever stayed in.
3 She plays tennis much better than I do.
4 Today isn't nearly as hot as it was yesterday.
5 These are the most expensive shoes I've ever bought.
6 This restaurant is far cheaper than the restaurant we normally go to.
7 That was the hardest exam I've taken in my life.
8 Yesterday evening she got home earlier than usual.

▶ **6.4**

1 He speaks more quickly than I do.
2 London is much more expensive than Edinburgh.
3 They make the best pizzas in Rome.
4 Colin is cleverer than his brother.
5 That was the saddest film I've ever seen.
6 The exam wasn't nearly as hard as I expected.
7 I think this is the simplest recipe in the book.
8 At the moment the weather in France is a little warmer than in the UK.

▶ **6.5**

A So, where do you think I should take my mother on holiday?
B If I were you, I'd take her somewhere warm, like Italy.
A You've been to Italy lots of times, haven't you? Where would you recommend taking her?
B Well, you should definitely go to Rome – it's such a beautiful city.
A That's a good idea. And when would you go?
B Er, let me see. Well, it's not a good idea to go in July or August, as it's much too hot for sightseeing then. It's much better to go in May or June, when it isn't quite as hot.
A And where do you think we should stay in Rome?
B Well, there are some lovely hotels in the centre, but they're at least 200 euros a night.
A You're kidding! I had no idea it would be that expensive. I can't afford to pay that much!
B Oh, well, in that case it's probably worth finding a hotel outside the centre, then.
A Yes, that makes sense. Thanks for your advice.

▶ **6.6**

1 You should definitely visit the British Museum when you're in London.
2 What dress would you wear to the party?
3 It's much better to take the train from London to Paris.
4 Would you recommend going to Athens in August?
5 It's probably worth booking a hotel before you go.
6 If I were you, I'd take the job in San Francisco.
7 Do you think I should buy this watch?
8 It's not a good idea to change your money at the airport.

▶ **6.7**

1 **A** My boyfriend's taking me to Paris this weekend!
    B Wow! That's amazing.
2 **A** I've been offered a place at Harvard University!
    B Oh, really? That's good.
3 **A** I got the best exam grades in my class!
    B That's amazing! Well done!
4 **A** My dad's going to buy me a rabbit!
    B Wow! That's brilliant.
5 **A** John's asked me to marry him!
    B Great! I'm so happy for you.
6 **A** We're going on holiday on Saturday!
    B I know. I can't wait!

▶ **6.8**

PEERAYA Hi Matt!
SYLVIE Hi!
MATT Hi Peeraya, how are you doing?
P Very well, thank you! This is my friend Sylvie, who I'm always talking about.
S Hi, Matt. Nice to finally meet you.
M Hi, Sylvie. You too. So, what are you two up to?
P Well, you know I said in my text message that our English course is almost over.
M Yeah, right. It's gone really quickly, hasn't it?
P It really has. Anyway, we're planning to celebrate with a meal out …
S Yes, but, uh, we don't really know Liverpool very well.
P So … we were sort of hoping you might be able to recommend some places to eat out?
S That would be really great.
M Yeah, sure. No problem at all. I mean, I'm not from Liverpool either but I've lived here for quite a few years now and so I think I know it pretty well. Um, OK, so how many people is the dinner for?
S Oh, uh, 18 I think?
P Yes, well. There are 18 students in our class but we'd like to invite our teachers, Phillipa and Sarah, too.
S Oh, yes, we definitely want them to come too.
M OK, so that's dinner for 20 people?
S Yes. Oh, actually, no. I've just remembered – Hiromi, one of the students, she wants to bring her husband, Shigeru. So that would be 21.
M OK, so you'll need quite a big restaurant then. There's nothing worse than waiting all night for one poor chef to try to prepare hundreds of starters and main courses.
P Yes, that's true!
S But, also, we'd like to go to a place that's, uh, how do you say this in English? Um, we don't want to go to a big company place. You know, one of those places like 'Star Noodles' or 'Wonderful Burgers' or any of those kinds of places. We want to go to a, you know, something more like a family restaurant.
M Yes, I know what you mean. You don't want to go to any chain restaurants.
S That's right! No chain restaurants.
M Sure. OK, so places to eat out. Hmm. Well, you should definitely look at restaurants in East Village. In fact, if I were you I'd go to The Thai House. It's a really nice restaurant and their seafood dishes are especially delicious. They're not too spicy but the food is always really fresh there.
P That sounds nice. But we were thinking that this is an English course, so we'd like to go to an English restaurant.
S Yes. I mean, do you know any places that do British food, or even better, food from Liverpool?
M Ah! I see what you mean –
P But not …
P/S Fish and chips!
M Don't worry! I knew what you meant. Well, it's probably worth going to Sarah's Bistro. They do a really good 'scouse'.
S 'Scouse'? What's that?
M It's a dish that's local to Liverpool. It's a kind of lamb stew, really tasty. Although you can get vegetarian scouse there now too.
P That sounds perfect!
S Yes, where is it?
M Well, do you know the traffic lights on the corner of Danielle Street and Porch Road?
P Yes.
M Well, you turn left there and go up Double Street until you see a cash machine. Turn right there and – you're there!
P Oh, thanks so much, Matt!
S Yes, thank you. That's great.
M No problem.

Unit 7

▶ 7.1

A Some new people have just moved into the house opposite.

B Yes, I know. I saw them yesterday when they arrived. I think they're French.

A No, they can't be French. Their car has a 'P' sticker on the back.

B Oh, really? They might come from Poland, then.

A Or they could be Portuguese?

B That's true – both countries begin with a 'P'.

A Is it a family or a couple?

B It must be a family. They must have two or three children.

A How do you know that?

B Because I saw some children's bikes in their garden. Also, there was another woman in the car when they arrived yesterday – she was older than the mother.

A She might be the children's grandmother.

B No, she can't be their grandmother. She only looked about 45.

A Or she could be their aunt? Or she might not be a relative at all. She may be just a friend. She might be helping them to unpack their things.

B Why don't we go and say 'hello'?

A But they might not speak English – it could be really embarrassing.

B They must speak English. I just saw them speaking to one of their neighbours and they seemed to understand each other.

▶ 7.2

1 He must have rich parents.
2 She can't be revising for her exams tonight.
3 They might enjoy going to the zoo.
4 You could invite Jenny to your party.
5 We must be quite near the centre now.
6 John must earn a lot more money than her.

▶ 7.3

1 **A** Do you think you could help me with the shopping bags?
   B Sure, I'll take them into the kitchen for you.
2 **A** Is there anything I can do to help?
   B Yes, there is, actually. Could you lay the table for me?
3 **A** Do you think I could have a quick shower?
   B Yes, of course. Let me get you a towel.
4 **A** May I use your phone?
   B Yes, of course. It's in the hall.
5 **A** Is it OK if I watch the news on TV?
   B Sure, no problem. Let me turn it on for you.
6 **A** Would you mind taking your shoes off?
   B No, not at all. Where shall I leave them?

▶ 7.4

1 Would you mind opening that door for me?
2 Is it OK if I leave my coat here?
3 **A** Do you think I could have a cup of tea?
   B Yes, of course. I'll make one for you.
4 **A** Would you mind if I used your toilet?
   B Not at all. Let me show you where it is.
5 Is there anything I can do to help?
6 Excuse me. Do you think you could turn the music down a little, please? It's really hard to talk in here.

▶ 7.5

1 a Would you mind getting me some more water?
   b Would you mind getting me some more water?
2 a Do you think you could lend me some money?
   b Do you think you could lend me some money?
3 a Is it OK if I make myself a coffee?
   b Is it OK if I make myself a coffee?
4 a Do you think I could borrow your car?
   b Do you think I could borrow your car?
5 a Do you mind if I make a quick phone call?
   b Do you mind if I make a quick phone call?

▶ 7.6

LUIS OK, is it my turn yet?

BEN Erm, not yet. You have to miss your turn this time because you only got three 'ones', remember?

L Oh, yes, I forgot. So whose turn is it now?

KATIA It's mine, yay!!! OK, come on, come on – be lucky! Give Katia the score she needs. OK, so I've got two 'sixes'. And what's that one? I can't see it from here.

B It's a 'four'.

K OK, so a 'four' and two 'sixes', sixteen. Is that good?

B Yes. You can move three places and you get – a 'Dream' question.

K Ooh! Excellent! Go on then.

B OK, 'You have one minute to describe your dream home to the other players – so just to Luis and Daniela – but not me. Every player has to draw what you describe – but with their eyes closed!'

L/DANIELA What? / No! / I can't draw to save my life!

B Yes, yes. Just take a pencil and be quiet. OK, Katia? Close your eyes, Luis! OK, so Katia, are you ready? Good! So, one minute from now!

K OK, so, my dream home! Let me see, oh OK, I know! I know! So, it would be in Moscow, right in the centre, in a fantastic location somewhere in a really nice neighbourhood near to Pushkin Square. OK, and it would have to be on the top floor of a really big building so that I could see the Kremlin and even Red Square from my window.

B What kind of building?

K A really big one.

B Yes, but what kind of building? Old? New?

K Oh, I see! OK, you're right, yes. OK, well, really new. Like from the 1990s or 2000s. In fact, from any time after 2010. So it would have lots of shiny metal and glass on the outside and lots of gold and marble on the inside. Because, actually, my dream home isn't a house but a luxury apartment. And it would be huge, I mean really, really big. And it would have a balcony along one side. The balcony would be really wide so that I'd have enough space for lots of flowers and a garden and a table where I could have picnics and parties. Oh, and actually, it would also have a big, a really, really big, square dance floor.

B What about inside the apartment? They have to draw that too!

L Oh man, you're kidding, right?

B No, no. And close your eyes!

L Uff!

K OK, inside the apartment would be completely different from the building. It would be decorated just like a room in an Irish country cottage. So, there would be lots of white walls and dark, brown wood. And really old things. The kitchen would have an old metal oven where I could make cakes and bread and things. And I'd also …

B Time's up! OK, Picasso, let's have a look at, oh …

Unit 8

▶ 8.1

SHOP ASSISTANT Good morning. Can I help you?

CUSTOMER 1 No, thank you. I'm just browsing.

CUSTOMER 2 So what kind of present do you want to buy for your nephew?

C1 I'm not really sure.

C2 It's difficult, isn't it? Let's have a look in the computer games section. I think they said on the radio that 'Mayhem 5' was going to come out this week.

C1 Yes, I think I heard that, too. Let's see if it's on sale.

C2 Look, there it is. €49.90.

C1 49.90! I can't afford that!

C2 You're right. That's a lot of money for a computer game. Let's have a look at the special offers over there. Here's one that's reasonably priced. It's from last year and it's only 19.99. That's a bargain, isn't it?

C1 Yes, that's good value for money. I'll buy him that one. I hope he doesn't already have it.

SA Don't worry. He can always take it back to his local store and change it for another one, or get a refund.

C1 OK, that's great. I'll take it, then.

▶ 8.2

1 To be honest, the film was kind of boring.
2 In my experience, Americans tend to be very friendly.
3 I don't normally like that kind of thing.
4 On the whole, I liked his new film.
5 Some of his songs can be rather depressing.
6 As a rule, Italian coffee is excellent.

▶ 8.3

1 He likes hip hop and rap music – you know, stuff like that.
2 We had a couple of days when it was cloudy and rainy, but on the whole we had pretty good weather.
3 Don't touch all that stuff in his office, please.
4 She likes watching documentaries about animals and nature and that sort of thing.

▶ 8.4

1 When did you last see her?
2 They went the wrong way and got lost.
3 Whose suitcase was the heaviest?
4 I wrote a long letter to my uncle in Scotland.
5 I didn't know which book to get my husband.
6 She had to wait two hours for the next train to London.

▶ 8.5

/h/: whose, heaviest, husband, had
/w/: when, went, way, which
First letter silent: wrong, wrote, hours

▶ 8.6

CATHY Hi, Cindy!

CINDY Hi, Cathy. How's it going?

CA Well, I've had better days.

CI Oh dear, what's happened?

CA Well, do you remember those boots I was looking at last week?

CI The brown leather ones?

CA Yes. Well anyway, yesterday I decided to go back and buy them.

CI Oh cool!

CA Ah, well …

CI Oh.

CA Yes, 'Oh'. I thought they were really good value when I bought them. I mean, fifty per cent off a pair of designer boots that had just come out only six months ago?

CI So what happened? Were they the wrong size or something?

CA That's what typically happens to me but no, not this time. When I got home and took them out of the box, I realised why they had fifty per cent off.

CI What do you mean?

CA As soon as I took them out of the box and turned them over, I saw that one of them had a big black mark on the side.

CI That's absolutely awful. I hope you took them back to the shop.

CA Yes, of course I did, but …

CI They didn't refuse to give you a refund, did they?

CA Ha! Yes, you've got it! I couldn't believe it!

CI I'm not surprised. But how …? I mean, what did they say?

CI Well, I went back to the shop and I found the manager and told him what had happened, that I'd been into the shop last week and tried on the boots and then I'd gone back yesterday to buy them. I couldn't see them on the shelves so I asked the assistant and he brought them out already in the box.

CI But didn't he show you the boots before you paid for them?

CA Well, yes he did. He took the top off the box and asked me if everything was OK but by that time, you see, the boots were already lying flat inside the box. So I could only see the good side of them. I didn't think to ask him to take them out of the box again.

CI Of course not. Why would you? So what did the manager say to that?

CA He told me that as a rule they would always give someone a refund but that that wasn't possible this time because they were in the sale.

CI You're kidding? So, what happened?

CA Well, he asked me if the shop assistant had shown me the boots in the box before I'd paid for them and I admitted that he had. But I said that I hadn't realised that they were on sale because there was something wrong with them. But again he just said that he was really sorry but he couldn't give me a refund.

CI Oh, what a …

CA I know.

CI So what's happening now?

CA To be honest, I don't know. Jim's suggested that I call a lawyer or something, but I'm not sure I want to go that far.

CI Oh, I'm sorry. That really is bad, isn't it?

CA I know, I know. So what would you recommend I do?

CI Well, how about …

Unit 9

▶ 9.1

1
When I was in London last summer I went to a superb concert during the BBC Proms, which is a festival of classical music at the Royal Albert Hall. It's great to hear a symphony or a concerto when it's performed by an orchestra of professional musicians who are playing live. They played symphonies by Mahler and Beethoven and there was also a huge choir of 80 people that sang Mozart's Requiem. At the end of the concert everyone in the audience stood up and gave the performers a standing ovation which lasted for over five minutes.

2
I've just heard on the radio that the band have been in the recording studio for the last month. They're making a new album of jazz, soul and blues songs, which they're bringing out in September. I've just listened to an amazing playlist of their old songs on the Internet. It's got about 30 tracks on it and most of them are old songs of theirs from the 80s and 90s.

▶ 9.2

1 Radio stations which have a lot of adverts are really annoying.
2 The band's fourth album, which they recorded in 2010, was their best so far.
3 The pianist, whose brother is also a musician, gave a superb performance.
4 In the article it says that people who eat healthily usually live longer.
5 Tickets for last year's festival, which my sister went to, cost €250!
6 I think operas which last more than three hours are really boring.

▶ 9.3

PAM Hi, Mel. Listen. Ian and I were thinking of going out for a meal this weekend. Would you guys like to come with us?

MEL Yes, that's a great idea. Where were you planning to go?

P We thought about going to that new Chinese restaurant in town. It's meant to be really good.

M Hang on a second. I'll just ask Tony … Sorry, Pam, but Tony isn't a big fan of Chinese food.

P OK, never mind. We could go somewhere else.

M Oh, I know. How about going to that new Italian restaurant near the station?

P Mmm, that sounds interesting.

M Yes, it's supposed to be excellent, and very good value for money.

P Yes, I'm sure Ian would like it. He loves pizzas and pasta.

M Good. Shall I book a table for Saturday evening?

P Yes, that would be perfect for us. Why don't we get a table for 8 o'clock?

M Yes, OK. I'll book one.

▶ 9.4

1 Sorry, but Sean isn't a big fan of science fiction films. What other films are on?
2 The new novel by JK Rowling, who wrote the Harry Potter books, is supposed to be really good.
3 The new animated film from Pixar has had great reviews in the papers.
4 **A** There's a documentary about the Roman occupation of Britain on TV tonight.
   B Really? That sounds interesting.
5 I'm not sure my father would be interested in going to an exhibition of surrealist paintings.
6 This hotel was recommended by a friend of mine, who stayed here last year.
7 That's a great idea. I'm sure Andy would love it.
8 The new Greek restaurant near my house is meant to be very good.

▶ 9.5

1 **A** Did you go to the concert with Luke?
   B No, I went with Will.
2 **A** Did James go to Edinburgh by bus?
   B No, he went on the train.
3 **A** So, your friend's a famous actor?
   B No, she's a famous dancer.
4 **A** So, you're from Lecce, in the south of Italy?
   B No, I'm from Lecco, in the north of Italy.
5 **A** Are you meeting your friend Pam on Thursday?
   B No, I'm meeting my friend Sam, on Tuesday.

▶ 9.6

DAVE OK, so that's the pizzas ordered.

MELISSA You remembered to get a vegetarian one for Greg and Kate, didn't you?

D Yes, yes. I got a vegetarian special. Oh, and there's plenty to drink for everyone too.

M Great. OK, so what film do we choose? This is supposed to be movie night after all.

D Well, let's have a look. Have you got all of them on your computer?

M Yes. I've downloaded a few, so we've got a good variety to choose from. Do you want to have a look with me so we can pick something?

D Sure, thanks. OK, so let's have a look. What's this, *Blackfish*? Is that a horror movie?

M Oh, no, it's a documentary. You haven't heard of it, then?

D Nope.

M Well, it's about the way killer whales are looked after in places like Sea World and Ocean World and that sort of thing.

D Oh, yeah?

M Yeah. It's an amazing film.

D So you've seen it already?

M Yeah, but I don't mind seeing it again.

D Hmm. Sounds a bit serious though. I mean I like documentaries but I think it would be better to watch something fun. What do you think?

M Hmm, yes you've got a good point there. OK, well we don't have to watch that one. It was just an idea.

D Great. So what about a comedy? Have you got any good ones?

LUCY Well, there's this one. It's quite old now but it's got Jim Carrey in it and he's usually quite funny, isn't he?

D Jim Carrey?

L Yeah, you know, um … Well anyway, *Man on the Moon* is supposed to be really good. Amazing performances, beautiful photography and a great story. I mean, it sounds really interesting and it was highly recommended by Professor Thomas.

D You mean your film studies lecturer?

L Yes, that's the one.

D Err, sounds a bit serious again. It says here that it's the biography of a comic actor but I'm not sure that it's actually a comedy. Yeah, look – most of the film is about the problems he had and about how he had to deal with a terrible illness. I'm not a big fan of films that are more intelligent than the audience, do you know what I mean? … You two really hate me now, don't you?

L No! Not yet.

M But I might do in a minute if you don't choose a film. Everyone will be here soon.

D OK, OK, just a moment. Hang on while I … There's *Star Wars*.

M/L No!

M I'm not really a fan of science fiction. And neither is Ofelia, or Rachel, or …

L Or Greg or Kate. Or me.

D OK, OK. Wait a minute. Oh! Oh! I've found it! I've found it! This is the one!

L *The Lego Movie*? Isn't that a cartoon?

M It's meant to be for kids, isn't it?

D Well, it is an animated film, but it's not just for kids. It's a comedy. And it's got some great songs. It's supposed to be really funny.

M Well …

D Will Ferrell does one of the voices.

M OK, then.

L Oh, OK then. Oh, have you got the cash for the pizza guy? Or do you need some more?

D Yes, I went to the bank earlier and …

Unit 10

▶ 10.1

1 I would go to the gym more often.
2 **A** Would he apply for a job in London?
   B No, he wouldn't.
3 She wouldn't lend you any money.
4 You wouldn't enjoy that film – it's too scary.
5 **A** Would you like to go for a pizza?
   B Yes, I would.

▶ 10.2

This is the story of how I met my wife Jane. It all started when I was going to work by taxi and it suddenly broke down. If my taxi hadn't broken down, I would've got to the station on time. If I'd arrived at the station on time, I wouldn't have missed my train. If I hadn't missed the train, I wouldn't have had to wait an hour for the next one. If I hadn't had to wait for an hour, I wouldn't have gone to the café for a coffee. If I hadn't had a coffee, I wouldn't have met my friend Sarah – and if I hadn't met Sarah, she wouldn't have introduced me to her friend Jane. So Jane and I met because my taxi broke down that morning!

▶ 10.3

1 If I hadn't fallen over, I wouldn't have hurt my knee.
2 We wouldn't have missed the bus if you had got up on time.
3 Julia would have passed her exams if she had worked harder.
4 If they had saved some money each week, they might have had enough to buy a car.
5 She would never have married him if she had known what a strange person he is.

▶ 10.4

A How do you feel about the party tonight, then?

B Er, I'm feeling OK …

A Good. Is everything ready?

B Yes, but I'm worried that not many people will come.

A You've got nothing to worry about. You've invited lots of people.

B Yes, but what if only a few people come?

A That's definitely not going to happen. Everyone I've spoken to says they're coming.

B Oh, good. You don't think we'll run out of food?

A No, I'm sure it'll be fine. You've made a lot of food and most people will probably bring something.

B Oh, OK, that's good.

▶ 10.5

1 That reminds me, what time does the match start?
2 Anyway, as I was saying, I'm worried about my exam.
3 You've got nothing to worry about.
4 Speaking of music, did you see *The X Factor* last night?
5 You don't think it will be a bit boring?
6 She's definitely going to like the ring.
7 I'm afraid that something will go wrong.
8 By the way, have you met his new girlfriend?

▶ **10.6**

1 **A** How much will an engagement ring cost?
   B About £500.
2 **A** How long has your sister known her boyfriend?
   B About four years.
3 **A** What time does the film start?
   B At half past eight.
4 **A** How often is there a train to York?
   B Every 45 minutes.
5 **A** How fast was the car going when the accident happened?
   B About 100 kilometres an hour.
6 **A** How much does it cost to fly to New York?
   B Around £600.

▶ **10.7**

PHIL Hi, Wendy! How's it going?
WENDY Mmm? Oh, hi Phil, it's you. Yeah, I'm doing OK. Not too bad.
P Hmm. You could try to sound more convincing when you say that!
W It's just … I had my interview this morning.
P Of course. How did it go?
W Awful. I want to be a doctor so much, but after that interview …
P Oh come on, I'm sure it wasn't that bad. You've got nothing to worry about with your marks.
W Thanks, I know. But I'm pretty sure they want more than just good grades. I mean, this is medical school. I read somewhere that for every place at university at least 10 people apply. There are so many people who are expecting me to get in to medical school. What do I do if I don't? I'd be so embarrassed.
P But you didn't just get good marks. You got the highest marks at school in every subject. If only I had grades like yours. And I'm sure you did your best. You always do! So anyway, what happened at your interview that you seem to think went so badly?
W Well, I was so nervous I could hardly speak. I must have sounded like a mouse.
P But they're expecting people to be nervous. Who was interviewing you?
W Oh, it was two senior doctors from the hospital plus a second-year medical student who's studying on the course now.
P Well, OK, but remember they've all done the same interview once. They must have understood how you were feeling.
W I don't know. Maybe. I'm still convinced that I did something wrong. Doctors have to be really confident, don't they? I mean they have to tell nurses what to do and they also have to make decisions that could mean life or death.
P Well, I suppose …
W And you can't be nervous when you're talking to a patient. I mean, can you imagine? If you were my patient and you said 'Oh, Doctor Wendy, do you think I'll be all right?' and then you'd hear me saying 'Oh, um, well, uh, I, uh, think you'll, um, be fine!'
P You don't sound like that.
W But –
P Listen to me, Wendy – you don't sound like that. I promise you. And anyway, what's the worst thing that can happen? OK, let's just imagine that you don't get a place at medical school this year –
W Oh!
P Just imagining! Anyway, what would you do?
W Um …
P OK, well I know what I'd do – I'd apply again next year and I'd take advantage of the time off to do something really interesting. In fact, I'd do something that I knew would help me in my interview next year.
W Like what?
P Well, you say you need more confidence, right? Well, do some research. Find out what you could do that will help you become more confident. I don't know, like, you could try acting. Yes, what about that? You could get a job during the day and then in the evenings you could take part in a play or something. And don't forget, that would only be if you didn't get a place on the medical course. Which you will, of course.
W Yeah, I suppose you're right. Thanks, that's really helpful. Actually, that reminds me, did you say there was something you wanted to ask me about?
P Ah, yes, I've got an interview at the Business School at the university next week and I wanted to ask you to give me some advice. I mean, I'm not sure what kind of questions they are going to ask me.
W Right, OK, well let's have a think …

Answer key

Unit 1

1A

1

a 2 hurts   3 happened   4 did they watch   5 did you talk   6 did he talk   7 got   8 did you vote

b 2 Which restaurant did your parents go to?
3 What happens to Harrison Ford at the end of the film?
4 What did you and your friends talk about?
5 What was your first mobile phone like?
6 What was his presentation about?
7 Which film star got married twice last year?
8 Who did you go to the cinema with?

2

a 2 presentation   3 joke   4 in touch   5 interviewed   6 expressing   7 in public   8 opinions

b 2 insisted   3 greeted   4 persuaded   5 encouraged   6 argue   7 persuaded   8 encouraged

1B

1

a 2 d   3 h   4 e   5 f   6 b   7 a   8 c

b 2 Is she studying   3 's learning   4 Does she want   5 doesn't know   6 's   7 Does she play   8 loves   9 is   10 's playing   11 's ringing   12 's waiting

2

a 2 e   3 a   4 c   5 b   6 d   7 h   8 g

b 2 freezing   3 tiny   4 miserable   5 impossible   6 filthy   7 delicious   8 useless

1C

1

a 1 **B** concerned   2 **A** guess **B** sure   3 **A** think **B** see   4 **A** opinion **B** mean

c 1 **B** mean   2 **A** I'm concerned **B** sure   3 **A** think **B** right   4 **A** opinion **B** where

2

a 1 **A** Guess what, <u>Tony</u>? I've just read about this <u>girl</u>, and she's only <u>ten</u> but she's fluent in several different languages.
   B That's <u>fantastic</u>. I can only speak one <u>language</u> – English.
2 **A** Hi, <u>Linda</u>. Are you learning Russian?
   B I'm trying to! But this book's <u>useless</u>! It teaches you how to say 'my uncle's black <u>trousers</u>' but not how to say 'hello'!

1D

1

a d

b True: 1, 4; False: 2, 3, 5

2

a 2 so that   3 This   4 This   5 in order   6 so

3

a **Suggested answer:**
How to improve your cookery skills

In order to become a good cook, the most important thing is to try new dishes and practise often. Most people usually cook the same dishes all the time. This means that they don't have the opportunity to improve their cookery skills by learning to cook new things.

It's a good idea to buy a few good recipe books so that you can learn how to cook some new dishes for the first time. At first, it's best to try cooking these new dishes for your family or one or two close friends only. This will make sure that you can cook them successfully before you cook them for a larger group of people at a dinner party. To become a confident cook, you should try cooking new recipes two or three times a week. Why not ask your family or friends to tell you what they really think of your food so that you can make it better the next time?

Another good way to improve your cookery skills is to watch cookery programmes on TV. It's usually easier to follow a recipe when someone shows you what to do. First you can watch the TV chef and then you can download the recipe from the TV channel's website.

Finally, each time you enjoy a good dish at a friend's house or at a restaurant, don't be afraid to ask for the recipe. This is the best way to discover new dishes and to become a better cook.

Reading and listening extension

1

a True: 2, 3, 5; False: 1, 4

b 2 d   3 c   4 a   5 g   6 f   7 b

2

a 1 c   2 a   3 b   4 b

b 2 Latin American studies   3 in Mexico   4 Another student   5 a city   6 absolutely perfect

Review and extension

1

2 My brother doesn't like coffee.
3 What was your holiday in Spain like? / How was your holiday in Spain?
4 Look at Tom – he's wearing his new shoes.
5 Who took you to the station?
6 Can you repeat that? I don't understand.

2

2 When we were young my brother and I used to argue all the time, but now we've become good friends.
3 It's impossible to sleep because my neighbours are having a party.
4 I haven't kept in touch with many of my old school friends. / I haven't stayed in touch with many of my old school friends.
5 That cake was delicious but there was only a tiny piece left!
6 My dad is very funny. He loves telling jokes about his time in the army.

3

a 2 Help   3 Enjoy   4 teach   5 look after   6 do

Unit 2

2A

1

a 1 **B** I've worked   2 **A** Have you ever arrived **B** I arrived   3 **A** Has she ever worked **B** she spent   4 **A** Matt's applied **B** hasn't had   5 **A** Have you met **B** I met

b 2 've worked   3 got   4 did you stay   5 stayed   6 did you like   7 enjoyed   8 gave   9 have you been   10 've been   11 have you had   12 joined   13 've been

2

a 2 c   3 b   4 f   5 h   6 a   7 d   8 g

b 2 charge   3 team   4 interview   5 CV   6 experience   7 grades   8 apply

3

2 b   3 b   4 a   5 b

2B

1

a 2 've been waiting   3 's been posting   4 've been reading   5 's been cooking   6 Have, been crying   7 have been learning   8 has, been going

b 2 I've installed   3 turned off   4 hasn't been working   5 You've been playing   6 been waiting   7 I've had   8 We've been trying

2

a 2 password   3 off   4 app   5 share   6 deleted   7 click   8 upload   9 typing   10 username

b Across: 6 install   7 browser   8 type
Down: 1 upload   2 message   4 connect   5 delete

2C

1

a 2 shame 3 taking 4 glad 5 talking 6 take 7 annoying 8 ask

c 2 What 3 worth 4 tried 5 give 6 Shall/Should 7 idea 8 let's
9 not 10 Can/Could

d 2, 10, 5, 9, 3, 7, 6, 1, 4, 8

2

a 2 My <u>boss</u> has been <u>criticising</u> my <u>work</u> recently.
3 My <u>neigh</u>bours had a <u>party</u> last <u>night</u> so I <u>didn't</u> <u>sleep</u> very <u>well</u>.
4 My computer's been <u>running</u> very <u>slowly</u> since I <u>installed</u> that new <u>program</u>.

2D

1

a c

b True: 1, 3, 6; False: 2, 4, 5

2

a 2 e 3 a 4 c 5 b 6 d

3

a **Suggested answer:**

Hi Martina

I'm sorry I haven't been in touch for the past few weeks but I've been incredibly busy.

I think I told you that I've been writing a story. I finished writing it a month ago and decided to send it to some publishing companies in London. Well, you'll never believe this but the editor of one of the biggest companies has just rung to offer me a contract.

They want me to make a few changes to the story so that it is more interesting for young people. I'm going to work closely with one of their editors who will make suggestions for improving the story. Besides helping me to improve the novel they're also going to pay me quite a lot of money. This means I can stop teaching and spend all of my time writing.

But the best thing is that they want me to go to New York to meet their American editors. I've never been to the USA before so I'm really looking forward to it. They think it might be possible to produce an American edition of the book. And what's really amazing is that they think my book could also become a film. Apart from meeting their American editors they also want me to meet some film producers from Hollywood!

What about having dinner together one day next week? There's a new Italian restaurant in the city centre that I'd like to try. Let me know a day that suits you.
Best wishes

Reading and listening extension

1

a 1 c 2 c 3 a 4 b

b 2 Dan 3 Neither 4 Kristen 5 Neither 6 Kristen 7 Dan 8 Neither
9 Kristen 10 Dan

2

a 6, 3, 5, 2, 4, 1

b 2 a 3 b 4 b 5 a 6 b

Review and extension

1

2 I can't talk to Julia because she's been speaking on the phone all day.
3 I went to Portugal on holiday three years ago.
4 I've known Jack for about five years.
5 His train was late this morning so he's just arrived.
6 Last night she went to the party with her sister.
7 He's been working as a taxi driver since 2008.
8 She's got red eyes because she's been crying.

2

2 Please turn off your phones as the film is about to start.
3 Can you give me your password so I can connect to the Internet?
4 I've got a lot of experience of managing people.
5 My brother just sent me a text message to say he'll be late.
6 Sarah applied for the job at the hospital but she didn't get it.
7 The English keyboard is different to the one in my language so I keep making mistakes when I type.
8 My brother has just got a new job with a large bank in London.

3

2 after 3 for 4 up 5 forward 6 interesting 6 around 7 out

Unit 3

3A

1

a 1 had started, made
2 was cleaning, fell, broke
3 had stopped, was
4 rang, was having
5 met, was working
6 saw, looked, had escaped
7 were talking, arrived

b 1 were studying
2 left, had cycled
3 arrived, had escaped
4 rode, took
5 heard, was watching
6 crashed, were crossing
7 had closed, got
8 called, was waiting

2

a 2 c 3 f 4 e 5 a 6 b

b 2 friendship 3 stranger 4 support 5 relatives 6 humour

3

a 2 They've got <u>lots of</u> <u>shared interests</u>.
3 He <u>gets on</u> very well with <u>his aunt</u>.
4 I'm not very <u>good at</u> <u>keeping in</u> touch with friends.
5 What does she <u>have in</u> common with <u>her American</u> cousin?

3B

1

a 2 usually walk
3 used to send
4 Did you used to get
5 didn't use to like
6 used to hang out
7 didn't use to have
8 Do you usually take

b 2 lives
3 used to drive
4 drives
5 used to go
6 goes
7 used to sit
8 sits
9 didn't use to eat
10 eats

2

a 2 nephew 3 childhood 4 middle 5 only 6 eldest 7 niece
8 generations

3

a 2 e 3 g 4 b 5 a 6 h 7 d 8 c

3C

1

a 2 Anyway 3 end 4 turned 5 guess 6 funny 7 won't 8 matters

c 2 The best thing is that it's got a swimming pool.
3 Anyway, we still had to find a present for Maggie.
4 To make matters worse, it started raining heavily.
5 You won't believe what I did on Saturday.
6 The funny thing was that she didn't realise what had happened.
7 In the end, he agreed to drive us to the station.
8 It turned out that she had lost her train ticket.

2

a 2 In the <u>end</u>, we went to a little restaurant near the <u>station</u>, where we had a lovely meal.

3 To make matters <u>worse</u>, the waiter dropped the bottle of <u>wine</u> and it ruined my new white dress.

4 On top of <u>that</u>, when she eventually got to the <u>airport</u> they told her that her flight was nearly two hours late.

5 <u>Anyway</u>, in the <u>end</u> I found a lovely flat in the <u>centre</u>, and the best thing <u>is</u> that it's only eight hundred euros a month!

b 2 In the <u>end</u> we went to a little <u>restaurant</u> near the station where we had a lo<u>vely</u> meal.

3 To make matters <u>worse</u>, the waiter dropped the bottle of <u>wine</u> and it <u>ru</u>ined my <u>new</u> <u>white</u> dress.

4 On top of <u>that</u>, when she eventually got to the <u>airport</u> they told her that her flight was nearly <u>two</u> hours late.

5 <u>Anyway</u>, in the <u>end</u> I found a lovely flat in the <u>centre</u>, and the <u>best</u> thing is that it's only <u>eight hundred</u> euros a month!

3D

1

a c

b True: 1, 4; False: 2, 3, 5

2

a 2 b   3 a   4 e   5 d   6 c

3

a **Suggested answer:**

My grandad's name was James Cooper and my sister and I were very fond of him. When we were children we used to go to my grandparents' house every Sunday for lunch. Grandad had a great sense of humour. He used to tell us terrible jokes and funny stories about his travels around the world.

James Cooper was born in London in 1928 and he had a very happy childhood. He had one brother and two sisters and they all got on very well. In 1936, his family moved to Montreal, in Canada, and he lived there for 10 years. He grew up speaking English and French fluently and in 1946 he returned to the UK to study medicine at Cambridge University. He graduated in 1952 and worked as a doctor in different hospitals in the UK from 1953 until 1962.

In 1962, he got a job at a hospital in San Francisco and lived in the USA for the next 13 years. While he was working there, he met Grandma and they got married in 1964. One year later, my mother was born. They didn't have any other children, so she was an only child. When my mother was 10, Grandad was offered a job in South Africa and so they all went to live in South Africa in 1975. They lived there for five years and they then returned to San Francisco in 1980. During their stay in Johannesburg, Grandad became good friends with the famous South African heart surgeon, Christiaan Barnard.

Grandad retired in 1988 and died 12 years later, in 2000. We all miss him very much.

Reading and listening extension

1

a 1 b   2 c   3 b   4 a   5 c

b 4, 2, 7, 8, 1, 5, 6, 3

2

a True: 4, 5, 6, 7; False: 1, 2, 3, 8

b 1 c   2 b   3 c   4 b   5 b   6 b

Review and extension

1

2 I used to have long hair when I was a little girl.

3 He was playing football when he fell over and hurt his ankle.

4 When he got to his house he was angry because someone had broken his window.

5 I got to the station five minutes late this morning and, unfortunately, my normal train had already left.

6 After the film we went to the café for a drink.

7 Did you use to play football when you were at school?

8 I didn't use to like English when I was at school.

2

2 Joanne's mother died when she was three so she was brought up by her grandparents.

3 I got to know Jasmine really well when we went travelling around South America together.

4 All my relatives got together at my dad's birthday party.

5 I don't have any brothers or sisters so I'm an only child.

6 She doesn't get on very well with her two brothers.

7 We share a lot of the same interests, for example literature.

8 My little brother's very calm and patient, so he takes after his mother because she's like that too.

3

2 time   3 lunch   4 idea   5 look   6 go

Unit 4

4A

1

a 2 Can you   3 he could   4 you'll be able to   5 was able to   6 couldn't   7 being able to   8 didn't manage to

b 2 f   3 d   4 c   5 a   6 e

2

a 2 ability   3 towards   4 determined   5 successful   6 gave up

b Across: 4 confident   5 successful   6 determined   7 talented
Down: 1 ability   2 bright   3 achievement

4B

1

a 1 the, Ø   2 a, Ø   3 Ø, Ø   4 a, the   5 an, the   6 Ø   7 Ø, a   8 the, the

b 2 I usually go to the gym three times a week.

3 Is there a supermarket opposite the bus stop near your house?

4 She usually goes to school on the Number 75 bus.

5 I often listen to the radio before I go to bed.

6 British pop groups are very popular in the USA.

7 There isn't an underground station near my hotel, so I'll have to take a taxi.

8 Usain Bolt was the fastest man in the world at the Olympic Games in 2012.

2

a 2 bored   3 terrifying   4 relaxing   5 disappointed   6 depressing   7 interested   8 satisfied

3

a 2 extrovert   3 sensitive   4 shy   5 sociable   6 talkative   7 introvert   8 serious

4C

1

a 2 e   3 f   4 c   5 g   6 d   7 b   8 a   9 i

2

a 1 **B** how **A** could   2 **B** something **A** hand **B** return
3 **A** favour **B** need **A** help **B** ask

3

a 2 ↘   3 ↘   4 ↗   5 ↗   6 ↘

4D

1

a 1 d   2 b

b True: 2, 4, 6; False: 1, 3, 5

2

a 2 h   3 f   4 b   5 a   6 c   7 e   8 d

3

a **Suggested answer:**

Summer camp coaches needed

Coaches are needed for a summer camp for children aged 5–12. Duties include organising indoor and outdoor activities for the children, helping them get ready for each day, have their meals and go to bed and entertaining them during their free time.

Candidates should be energetic and enthusiastic with an outgoing personality. A sense of adventure, a sense of humour and a positive attitude are essential. Candidates should be good at sports and ideally have a talent for art. Our summer camp coaches should love working with children and should be able to get on well with all the other members of the team.

Candidates should be aged 18 or over and preferably be university students or graduates. No previous experience is required. All new staff will be required to attend a two-day training course.

Candidates should complete the online application form and include an up-to-date CV. You will be contacted by our Human Resources Department to discuss potential opportunities.

Reading and listening extension

1

a 1 a   2 b   3 c   4 c

b True: 1, 3, 5, 6;   False: 2, 4, 7

2

a 1 b   2 b   3 c   4 c

b Possible answers
2 Bread was the most important part of most people's diet.
3 Frederick thought that if people had potatoes, they would not be hungry any more.
4 People in Kolberg said their animals could not eat potatoes.
5 People understood that potatoes were valuable when they saw the soldiers around Frederick's garden.
6 People began stealing potatoes from Frederick's garden.
7 Frederick's plan was successful.
8 Frederick's plan was an example of good psychology.

Review and extension

1

2 When she goes to the cinema she doesn't like seeing horror films.
3 Will you be able to help me with my maths homework this evening? / Can you help me with my maths homework this evening?
4 I love watching documentaries about whales.
5 She would like to be able to play the piano as well as her sister.
6 He usually gets to work at about 8.30 in the summer.
7 We weren't able to find the restaurant so we went to the pizzeria instead.
8 It's one of the best shopping websites on the Internet.

2

2 We had a very relaxing holiday in the South of France.
3 The film was so boring that I nearly fell asleep.
4 My uncle was a very successful businessman in the 1960s.
5 My sister doesn't want to watch the match because she isn't very interested in sport.
6 I thought that documentary about the environment was rather depressing.

3

2 so far   3 or so   4 and so on   5 such   6 so tired

Unit 5

5A

1

a 2 g   3 a   4 b   5 h   6 e   7 d   8 c

b 1 **B** Yes, good idea. I'll phone the pizzeria to book a table.
2 **A** What time is your brother arriving? / What time is your brother going to arrive? / What time will your brother arrive?
  B This evening. I'll drive to the station to meet him at 6.30. / I'm going to drive to the station to meet him at 6.30.
3 Hello, John. The traffic's really bad in the centre. We'll be about 20 minutes late. / We're going to be about 20 minutes late.
4 In my opinion the next president of the USA will be a Republican. / In my opinion the next president of the USA is going to be a Republican.
5 Shall I help you bring in the shopping from the car?
6 **A** What time are you having your hair cut this afternoon? / What time are you going to have your hair cut this afternoon?
7 I don't think Brazil will win the football match tomorrow. / I don't think Brazil is going to win the football match tomorrow.
8 **B** I don't know. Perhaps he'll get a job in that new hotel at the beach. / Perhaps he's going to get a job in that new hotel at the beach.

2

a 2 e   3 d   4 c   5 b

b 2 climate   3 pollution   4 environmentally   5 destroyed
6 endangered   7 wildlife   8 conservation

3

a /eɪ/: save, danger, education, nature
/ɑː/: plant, park, after, branch
/æ/: charity, animal, mammal, dam
/ə/: local, abroad, gorilla, along

5B

1

a 2 We'll phone you when our plane lands at Glasgow Airport.
3 If we don't stop hunting tigers, they'll be extinct in 20 years' time.
4 When the weather gets too cold, the birds fly south.
5 My dad will buy me a new laptop if I help him paint the house.
6 If you feel hungry later, have a banana or an apple.
7 I'll be there at 11 o'clock unless there's a problem with the train.
8 Unless the bus comes soon, I'm going to take a taxi.

c 1 they'll be   2 see, give   3 goes, changes   4 Unless, won't be able to
5 Open, feel   6 she misses, will have to   7 goes, usually feels
8 won't be able to, send

2

a 2 fur   3 paws   4 feathers   5 tail   6 petal   7 branch   8 web   9 scales

b Across: 4 sea   5 oceans   7 desert   9 waterfalls
Down: 2 rainforest   3 lake   6 streams   8 cave

5C

1

a 2 like   3 due to   4 **B** Such as **A** for instance   5 so   6 Since   7 As a result
8 because of

2

a 2 Well   3 question   4 second

3

a 2 pear   3 cap   4 bloom   5 cup

5D

1

a 1 First of all   2 Secondly   3 Finally   4 In conclusion

b c

c True: 2, 3, 5; False: 1, 4

2

a Suggested answer:

Getting our energy from the sun

If you think that you spend too much money on electricity, you might consider buying solar panels for your house. So, what are the advantages of solar panels?

Firstly, solar panels are a very efficient way of producing energy and they are very good for the environment. They don't pollute the atmosphere with carbon dioxide or other harmful gases. If you live somewhere with plenty of sunshine, they will generate all the electricity you need for a family home.

Secondly, although they aren't cheap to buy or install, they will eventually save you a lot of money on your electricity bills. Also, if you produce more electricity than you need, your energy company will pay you for the extra electricity. As a result, you will earn extra money if you have solar panels.

Finally, solar panels can increase the value of your home. If your house has solar panels on the roof, people will usually pay a higher price because they know that they will save money on their electricity bills.

In conclusion, I would say that it is a very good idea to buy solar panels for your house. It is environmentally friendly and it will give you cheaper electricity for many years.

Reading and listening extension

1

a A 4 B 6 C 5 D 3

b 1 b 2 a 3 a 4 b 5 b 6 a 7 b

2

a 3, 5, 2, 4, 1

b True: 2, 5, 6; False: 1, 3, 4

Review and extension

1

2 If he arrives before 2.00, we'll take him to that Italian restaurant for lunch.
3 Wait! I'll help you do the shopping if you like.
4 Unless it rains this afternoon, we'll play golf.
5 I can't come with you because I'm playing tennis with Joe this afternoon. We're meeting at the tennis club at 3.00.
6 If they win the next game, they'll win the gold medal.

2

2 There are fantastic beaches on the coast near Rio de Janeiro.
3 It hardly ever rains in the desert.
4 Air pollution is a serious problem in big cities like Tokyo.
5 The leaves of that tree are as big as my hand.
6 She's working on a very important project to save endangered species from extinction.

3

2 fix 3 causes 4 tackle 5 are aware of 6 facing

Unit 6

6A

1

a 2 mustn't 3 ought to 4 don't have to 5 can 6 must 7 can't
8 shouldn't

c 2 b 3 a 4 e 5 d 6 c

2

a 2 d 3 f 4 b 5 a 6 e

3

a 2 out 3 up 4 around 5 up 6 around 7 back 8 away

4

a 2 <u>rush</u> hour 3 <u>wash</u>ing machine 4 <u>cycle</u> lane 5 <u>lunch</u>time
6 <u>cash</u> machine

6B

1

a 2 This is by far the most luxurious hotel I've ever stayed in. / This is the most luxurious hotel I've ever stayed in by far.
3 She plays tennis much better than I do.
4 Today isn't nearly as hot as it was yesterday.
5 These are the most expensive shoes I've ever bought.
6 This restaurant is far cheaper than the restaurant we normally go to. / The restaurant we normally go to is far cheaper than this restaurant.
7 That was the hardest exam I've taken in my life.
8 Yesterday evening she got home earlier than usual. / She got home earlier than usual yesterday evening.

c 2 London is much more expensive than Edinburgh.
3 They make the best pizzas in Rome.
4 Colin is cleverer than his brother.
5 That was the saddest film I've ever seen.
6 The exam wasn't nearly as hard as I expected.
7 I think this is the simplest recipe in the book.
8 At the moment the weather in France is a little warmer than in the UK.

2

a 2 cooked 3 raw 4 crunchy 5 creamy 6 sour 7 fresh 8 heavy

b 2 mash 3 chop, fry 4 Add 5 mix, serve 6 Heat up, stir

6C

1

a 2 were 3 recommend 4 definitely 5 would 6 idea 7 better 8 should
9 kidding 10 worth

c 2 wear 3 to take 4 going 5 booking 6 I'd 7 should 8 to change

2

a 2 bored 3 excited 4 excited 5 bored 6 excited

6D

1

a 1 A 2 B 3 A 4 A

b True: 1, 5, 6; False: 2, 3, 4

2

a 2 rather 3 a bit 4 rather small 5 extremely 6 completely 7 reasonably
8 terribly

3

a Suggested answer:

Last Saturday I took my girlfriend to Chez Pierre for her birthday. It's a new French restaurant in the city centre. The atmosphere was really relaxing and although there was classical and French music it wasn't very loud so it was easy to talk. The waiters were extremely friendly and the service was good. Our fish was absolutely delicious and the salad was very fresh and tasty. For dessert I had a lovely apple tart with cream and Anna had ice cream. All the portions were extremely generous and although the meal was rather expensive I would definitely recommend going there for a special occasion.

A friend of mine recommended the *Villa Borghese* restaurant to us. It's an Italian restaurant just by the beach and they serve mostly Italian food such as pizzas and pasta. Unfortunately, it was a bit disappointing. The restaurant was extremely noisy because there were lots of young children and loud pop music so it was rather difficult to talk. Because of this, the atmosphere wasn't very relaxing. We went on a Friday evening and the restaurant was completely full but there weren't enough waiters. The service was awful – we were there for nearly an hour before anyone took our order. We ordered pasta but it was rather overcooked and the sauce wasn't very tasty. Our meal was fairly cheap but the food wasn't very good so I definitely wouldn't go there again.

Reading and listening extension

1

a True: 1, 4; False: 2, 3

b 1 a 2 b 3 c 4 b 5 a 6 c

2

a 1 c 2 b 3 a 4 a

b 2 for quite a long time 3 21 4 chain 5 traditional English dishes
6 meat dish 7 turn right

Review and extension

1

2 I think this is the best Greek restaurant in London.
3 Last night we had to take a taxi because we'd missed the bus.
4 His house is nearer the university than yours.
5 You mustn't park outside that school.
6 He's taller than his older brother.
7 You mustn't feed the animals in the zoo – it's forbidden.
8 I think French is easier to learn than English.

2

2 Can I borrow your spoon so I can stir my coffee?
3 We had three hours to wait so we looked round the old town.
4 The best way to get around New York is to take the subway.
5 Squeeze the lemon and pour the juice over the fish.
6 If you put in too much sugar, it will be too sweet to drink.

3

2 f 3 c 4 b 5 a 6 e

Unit 7

7A

1

a 2 e 3 a 4 c 5 f 6 d 7 b

b 2 might 3 could 4 must 5 must 6 might 7 can't 8 could 9 might not
10 may 11 might 12 might not 13 could 14 must

2

a Across: 6 neighbourhood 7 view 8 floor
Down: 1 location 3 balcony 4 basement 5 doorbell

b 2 rented, flat 3 landing, floor 4 front, locks 5 out of, into 6 ground, terrace

3

a Final /t/ or /d/: 3, 4, 6

7B

1

a 1 some 2 enough 3 too many 4 plenty 5 a few 6 no 7 enough
8 little

b 2 Unfortunately, there aren't any good restaurants near here. / Unfortunately,
there are no good restaurants near here.
3 He won't pass his exams because he hasn't worked hard enough this year.
4 **A** Is there any milk left? / Is there much milk left?
  B Yes, we've got plenty.
5 There were too many people at the bus stop to get on the bus.
6 There are too few eggs in the fridge to make a Spanish omelette. / There
aren't enough eggs in the fridge to make a Spanish omelette.
7 My father's too old to play tennis these days.
8 She made a lot of mistakes in her translation. / She made lots of mistakes in
her translation.

2

a 2 about 3 for 4 about 5 on 6 about 7 with 8 in

b 2 cope with 3 apologised to 4 rely on 5 worried about 6 belongs to
7 complained about 8 argued with

7C

1

a 2 f 3 e 4 c 5 a 6 b

c 2 really 3 Sure 4 control 5 lovely 6 better

d 2 leave 3 **A** I could **B** I'll 4 **A** I used **B** Let 5 anything 6 could

2

a 2 b 3 b 4 a 5 a

7D

1

a c

b True: 3, 4; False: 1, 2, 5

2

a 2 There's a good shop at the end of my road. Alternatively / Otherwise / Apart
from that, you could go to the huge supermarket which is just before you get
to the motorway.
There's a good shop at the end of my road. Another option / Another
possibility is to go to the huge supermarket which is just before you get to the
motorway.
3 You can get a good view of London from the London Eye. Alternatively /
Otherwise / Apart from that, you can go to the top of The Shard building.
You can get a good view of London from the London Eye. Another option /
Another possibility is to go to the top of The Shard building.
4 I suggest you go to the beach early in the morning, before it gets too hot.
Alternatively / Otherwise / Apart from that, you could go late in the afternoon.
I suggest you go to the beach early in the morning, before it gets too hot.
Another option / Another possibility is to go late in the afternoon.
5 Why don't you go to that Italian restaurant opposite Covent Garden
Underground Station? Alternatively / Otherwise / Apart from that, you could
try that new Japanese restaurant near Leicester Square.
Why don't you go to that Italian restaurant opposite Covent Garden
Underground Station? Another option / Another possibility is to try that new
Japanese restaurant near Leicester Square.

3

a Suggested answer:

Hi Pascale

Thanks for babysitting for us this evening. Hope you get on well with the
children and that everything goes well. Here are some suggestions for the
evening.

Please make yourself at home and help yourself to hot drinks and a snack.
There is some tea and coffee by the kettle. Otherwise, you can make some hot
chocolate. It's in the cupboard on the right of the fridge. There are plenty of
chocolate biscuits on the table. Alternatively, there's some delicious cheesecake
in the fridge.

Can you give the children their dinner at around 7 o'clock? In the fridge there's
some chicken soup and fish pie. You can cook this in the microwave. Another
option is to make them some sandwiches. You'll find plenty of cheese in the
fridge and there's also some apple juice.

After that, you could watch something on TV with them. They both love
watching *The X Factor*. Otherwise you could watch one of their favourite DVDs
with them, such as *Pirates of the Caribbean* or *Toy Story*. All the DVDs are on
the bookcase next to the TV.

By the way, they usually go to bed at about 9 o'clock. You can read them a
bedtime story. You'll find plenty of books on the bookcase in their bedroom.
They both love the *Harry Potter* books. Another possibility is to start reading
The Lion, the Witch and the Wardrobe with them. I think they might enjoy it.

Finally, if you have any problems, please phone me on my mobile
(07700 900221). Alternatively, you can call my husband's/wife's mobile
(07700 900834).

Hope you have a good evening and see you around 11.30.

Reading and listening extension

1

a A 6 B 1 C 5 D 3

b 9, 7, 8, 2, 4, 1, 5, 3, 10, 6

2

a 2 f 3 a 4 e 5 c 6 b

b 1 c 2 c 3 c 4 c 5 a 6 c 7 b 8 c

Review and extension

1

2 George isn't good enough at football to play for the school team.
3 She can't be the manager – she looks too young!
4 There's a lot of traffic / There's lots of traffic in the town centre during the rush
hour.
5 They can't be doing their homework at this moment – it's nearly midnight!
6 The maths exam was too difficult for most of the people in my class.

2

2 She complained to the waiter about the dirty glass.
3 I can't afford to buy a flat at the moment so I'm going to rent a flat in the city
centre.
4 Don't worry about the bill. I'll pay for the meal.
5 I live in a really nice neighbourhood – everyone's very friendly.
6 When he told me about the accident, I didn't believe him at first.

3

2 c 3 a 4 f 5 e 6 d

Unit 8

8A

1

a 2 She said I should wait behind the line until it was my turn.
3 When I met her last Friday she asked me if I was going to Harry's party the next day.
4 She told me (that) he might be about fifty years old.
5 He told me he was sorry but he couldn't come to my party that evening. / He said he was sorry but he couldn't come to my party that evening.
6 She asked me if I had seen my uncle when I was in New York last year. / She asked me whether I had seen my uncle when I was in New York last year. / She asked me if I had seen my uncle when I was in New York the year before. / She asked me whether I had seen my uncle when I was in New York the year before.
7 He told Anna he would see her next week. / He told Anna he would see her the following week.

b 2 He said that Martin had just sent him a text message.
3 He told me that he would phone me when he got back from work.
4 He asked me if I was going to buy my brother a present that afternoon. / He asked me whether I was going to buy my brother a present that afternoon.
5 She asked me why I couldn't lend her some money.
6 The examiner said that we had to stop writing immediately and give him / her our papers.
7 She told me she wanted me to take the flowers for my grandmother.

2

a 2 news 3 entertainment 4 spread 5 celebrity gossip 6 organisation 7 current 8 political

b Across: 6 presenter 7 breaking 8 posted
Down: 1 headline 2 article 3 reporter 5 business

8B

1

a 1 going 2 seeing 3 to get 4 to come 5 visiting 6 waiting 7 going, to see 8 paying

b 2 Don't forget to give me back my book when you've finished reading it.
3 He admitted stealing the old lady's handbag.
4 We hoped to find a good place to eat in one of the streets near the station.
5 He threatened to tell my parents what I had done.
6 It's really important to teach your children how to cross the road safely.
7 She didn't know which book to buy her brother for his birthday.
8 You promised to help me with my homework!

2

a 2 come 3 sale 4 afford 5 priced 6 bargain 7 value 8 back 9 refund

3

a 2 agreed 3 suggested 4 warned 5 refused 6 offered

8C

1

a 2 In my experience, Americans tend to be very friendly.
3 I don't normally like that kind of thing.
4 On the whole, I liked his new film.
5 Some of his songs can be rather depressing.
6 As a rule, Italian coffee is excellent.

2

a 2 couple, whole 3 stuff 4 sort

3

a/b /h/: whose, heaviest, husband, had
/w/: when, went, way, which
First letter silent: wrong, wrote, hours

8D

1

a d

b True: 1, 4; False: 2, 3, 5

2

a 2 I heard a story on the radio about an elephant which, apparently, sat on a car in a safari park.
3 The 12-year-old girl stole her father's motorbike and rode it for 40 km along the motorway before the police stopped her near Oxford. / The 12-year-old girl stole her father's motorbike and rode it for 40 km along the motorway but the police stopped her near Oxford.
4 The woman hit the teenager hard on his head with her umbrella. Then she used his mobile phone to call the police. / The woman hit the teenager hard on his head with her umbrella and then used his mobile phone to call the police. / The woman hit the teenager hard on his head with her umbrella before using his mobile phone to call the police. / The woman hit the teenager hard on his head with her umbrella and then called the police with his mobile phone. / The woman hit the teenager hard on his head with her umbrella before calling the police with his mobile phone.
5 Amanda escaped from the burning building by breaking a window with her shoe.
6 There was an incredible story on the news about a baby in China who fell from a fourth-floor window but she wasn't hurt because a man in the street caught her.

3

a **Suggested answer:**

Hi Martina

There was an incredible story on the Internet today about a car which crashed into a family's house in Manchester. Apparently, Richard and Judy Knowles and their children were watching TV when suddenly they heard a loud noise. The driver of the car had lost control of his car and had driven straight through the front door of the house before stopping two metres from the kitchen. Amazingly, no one in the house nor in the car was seriously hurt. It seems that the family of four and their dog were all in the living room at the time of the accident. When they realised what had happened, they immediately called the police, who arrived at the scene five minutes later. The front of the house was badly damaged but, fortunately, the driver of the car and his three passengers only suffered minor injuries. It took the fire service six hours to remove the vehicle from the house.

Reading and listening extension

1

a 1 c 2 c 3 b 4 b

b 2 Frankie 3 Neither 4 Frankie 5 Neither 6 Frankie 7 Mercedes 8 Frankie 9 Neither 10 Mercedes 11 Frankie 12 Mercedes

2

a True: 2, 3, 4, 7; False: 1, 5, 6, 8

b 1 b 2 a 3 a 4 b 5 c 6 b

Review and extension

1

2 They asked me if I was going to the football match. / They asked me whether I was going to the football match.
3 He has agreed to take us to the airport.
4 When I phoned him last night, he said he had just finished his exams.
5 She advised me not to tell anyone about our meeting.
6 Yesterday he said he would help me with my homework. / Yesterday he told me he would help me with my homework.
7 I'm really looking forward to seeing you on Sunday.

2

2 The new song by Rihanna is going to come out next week.
3 My sister likes reading the celebrity gossip pages in the Sunday paper.
4 He advised me to buy a new laptop because mine is over five years old.
5 I don't usually watch programmes about politics on TV.
6 She remembered to book a table at the restaurant. / She reminded me to book a table at the restaurant.
7 The main headline on the front page of my newspaper today is BARACK WINS U.S. ELECTION.

3

2 on 3 on 4 in 5 in 6 on 7 in 8 in

Unit 9

9A

1

a 2 *Saving Private Ryan* was directed by Steven Spielberg in 1998.
3 The actors have been told to come back at 15.00.
4 1,000 films are made in Bollywood every year.
5 The movie *Avatar* was seen by 35 million people in its first two weeks. / The movie *Avatar* was seen in its first two weeks by 35 million people.
6 The prime minister is being interviewed on TV at this very moment. / The prime minister is being interviewed at this very moment on TV.
7 200,000 cars are produced by our new factory every year. / 200,000 cars are produced every year by our new factory.
8 CGI is being used to create the special effects.

b 2 Five different varieties of orange are grown in this region.
3 Students will be given a loan to pay for their university fees by the government. / Students will be given a loan by the government to pay for their university fees.
4 The special effects are being created with the latest animation software.
5 The actors have been asked to give some of their fees to charity.
6 The car was being driven really fast when the accident happened.
7 The pop star was asked about his new album by the journalist. / The pop star was asked by the journalist about his new album.
8 The president was given a big bunch of flowers by a little girl in a pink dress.

2

a 2 horror 3 thriller 4 science fiction 5 game show 6 documentary
7 animated 8 chat show 9 action 10 soap opera

b Across: 4 character 5 based on
Down: 1 director 3 scene 6 studio

9B

1

a 2 While you're in Italy you should visit the town of Verona, where there is a lovely Roman amphitheatre.
3 John Lennon, who was a member of the pop group The Beatles, was murdered in 1980.
4 Pelé, whose real name is Edson Arantes do Nascimento, was a famous Brazilian footballer.
5 Steven Spielberg was the director of the film *Saving Private Ryan*, which was about a group of American soldiers in the Second World War.
6 First we went to Paris, where we visited the Eiffel Tower, and then we took the train to Lyon.
7 In my view, Bruce Springsteen's best album is *The River*, which he recorded in 1980.
8 Bill Clinton, who was President of the USA from 1993 to 2001, is giving a talk at our university next month.

2

a 2 performed 3 orchestra 4 musicians 5 live 6 choir 7 audience
8 recording 9 album 10 playlist 11 tracks

3

a 2 performance 3 charity 4 development 5 happiness 6 creativity
7 celebration 8 culture

4

a 2 non-defining 3 non-defining 4 defining 5 non-defining 6 defining

9C

1

a 2 Would 3 come 4 that's 5 to go 6 thought 7 meant 8 Hang 9 of
10 else 11 going 12 sounds 13 supposed 14 would like 15 Shall
16 don't

c 2 supposed 3 reviews 4 **B** sounds 5 sure, interested 6 recommended
7 idea, love 8 meant

2

a 1 No, I went with <u>Will</u>.
2 No, he went on the <u>train</u>.
3 No, she's a famous <u>dancer</u>.
4 No, I'm from <u>Lecco</u>, in the <u>north</u> of Italy.
5 No, I'm meeting my friend <u>Sam</u>, on <u>Tuesday</u>.

9D

1

a b

b True: 1, 4, 5; False: 2, 3

2

a 2 Although 3 However 4 Despite 5 While 6 Although 7 Despite
8 In spite of

3

a **Suggested answer:**

Why I prefer reading a book

I love going to the cinema and I have seen a lot of films which are based on famous books. However, I normally prefer reading the original book to seeing the film version.

The first reason for enjoying the book more than the film is because a book usually takes several days or weeks to read whereas a film only lasts for two or three hours. So I can enjoy reading a book for much longer than watching a film. Furthermore, because most films are much shorter than books, the director has to cut a lot of the interesting details from the story. As a result, films only show the most important scenes of the story and don't usually tell the audience what the characters are thinking.

Another reason I prefer the book is that when you are reading a story you have to use your imagination. The reader imagines what the people and the places in the story look like and how the characters speak. However, this isn't possible when you watch a film because the director makes the decisions about the appearance of the characters and the scenes.

Finally, reading a book is a great way to relax and to enter the world that the author has created. You can read a book anywhere you like – in bed, on the beach or on a train as you travel to work. While it is true that these days you don't have to watch a film at the cinema or on TV, it is still much easier to take a book with you and read a chapter when you have nothing else to do for half an hour.

So, although it is much easier to watch the film adaptation of a novel than to read the original book, I prefer reading the book. It lasts longer and gives me more enjoyment, it allows you to use your imagination and it is a very good way to relax.

Reading and listening extension

1

a True: 2, 3, 5; False: 1, 4, 6

b 1 d 2 d 3 b 4 c 5 a

2

a 1 b 2 c 3 c 4 a

b 2 computer 3 documentary 4 serious 5 performances 6 comedy
7 animated

Review and extension

1

2 A new bridge is being built at the moment by a Chinese construction company.
3 I interviewed the actor that had just won an Oscar.
4 *Sunflowers* was painted by Vincent Van Gogh.
5 Where is the new James Bond film being made?
6 He's the player that used to be in our team.

2

2 The actor was annoyed because someone in the audience had forgotten to switch off his mobile phone.
3 My father's a professional musician who plays the clarinet in the London Philharmonic Orchestra.
4 In *Titanic*, Leonardo DiCaprio plays a character who falls in love with the daughter of an American millionaire.
5 When I was about sixteen I saw The Rolling Stones play live at a festival in Germany.
6 I'm not very keen on horror films like *Dracula*.

3

2 Have you seen my brother? He said he'd meet me here.
3 I don't see why you're so angry with us.
4 She always listens to pop music in her bedroom.
5 I'm seeing my grandparents next Sunday.
6 Sorry, this phone's terrible. I can't hear you very well.
7 I've finished this exercise. Please look at it for me.

Unit 10

10A

1

a 1 'd be able to / could   2 'd take, were   3 'd go, lived   4 spoke, 'd apply
5 'd like, knew   6 'd learn, didn't have   7 would buy, could / were able to
8 wouldn't be, beat

b 1 'll pay   2 trained, 'd be   3 don't lose, 'll be   4 'd be, had
5 didn't live, 'd visit   6 'll come, finish

2

a 1 score   2 lost   3 didn't win, missed   4 beat   5 have a go   6 track

3

a 2 essential for   3 interested in   4 good at   5 similar to   6 worried about
7 scared of

4

a 2 **A W B** S   3 S   4 S   5 **A W B** S

10B

1

a 1 hadn't fallen
2 wouldn't have been able to, I'd lost
3 wouldn't have married, she'd known
4 hadn't, mightn't have
5 wouldn't have, hadn't
6 hadn't read, wouldn't have found
7 would have won, hadn't missed
8 hadn't started, could have finished

b 2 would've got / would have got   3 'd arrived   4 wouldn't have missed
5 hadn't missed   6 wouldn't have had to   7 hadn't had to
8 wouldn't have gone   9 hadn't had   10 wouldn't have met   11 hadn't met
12 wouldn't have introduced

2

a 2 f   3 a   4 b   5 d   6 e

b 2 made   3 take   4 doing   5 made   6 take   7 doing

3

a 1 W   2 W, S   3 S, W

10C

1

a 2 feeling   3 worried   4 nothing   5 about   6 what if   7 definitely   8 happen
9 think   10 it'll

c 2 Anyway, as I was saying, I'm worried about my exam.
3 You've got nothing to worry about.
4 Speaking of music, did you see *The X Factor* last night?
5 You don't think it will be a bit boring?
6 She's definitely going to like the ring.
7 I'm afraid that something will go wrong.
8 By the way, have you met his new girlfriend?

2

a 2 U   3 U   4 S   5 U   6 S

10D

1

a a

b True: 2, 4; False: 1, 3, 5, 6

2

a 2 would   3 definitely   4 pretty   5 better   6 expect   7 should   8 suggesting

3

a Suggested answer:

Positive reply:

Hi Jane

That's brilliant news about your exams! Congratulations!

I think you should definitely accept your dad's offer of a job. I'm pretty sure you'd enjoy working in one of his hotels as a trainee manager. You'd probably become a hotel manager in a few years' time and that would be fantastic. Also, I think it would be better to take a job now instead of going to university for three years. It might be hard to find a job when you finish in three years' time. I think this could be an excellent opportunity for you, so, if I were you, I'd go for it.

Let me know what you decide to do.

Speak soon

Careful reply:

Hi Jane

That's brilliant news about your exams! Congratulations!

I'm not sure what I think about your dad's offer. I can see that it would be exciting to train as a hotel manager but, if I were you, I'd think about it very carefully before making a decision.

I expect you'd enjoy working in one of your dad's hotels, but you also need to think about your career. Maybe it would be better to go to university and get a degree before you start working in a permanent job? If you take a degree in Business Studies, you'll be able to apply for jobs in lots of different areas of business after you graduate. On the other hand, if you start working in the hotel industry now, you might find that it's hard to get into another area in the future. I'm just suggesting that it might be better to go to university first and then decide what you want to do after you graduate.

Let me know if you want to meet up and talk about it.

Speak soon

Reading and listening extension

1

a 2 Luis   3 Dean, Luis   4 Stevo, Micky   5 Pilar

b True: 1, 4, 5, 6, 7; False: 2, 3, 8

2

a 1 Wendy   2 Wendy   3 Phil   4 Wendy   5 Phil   6 Phil

b 1 b   2 a   3 a   4 a   5 a   6 c

Review and extension

1

2 If there hadn't been an accident, we wouldn't have missed our flight.
3 If I were you, I'd wait until the shop has a sale to buy a jacket.
4 She wouldn't have failed her exam if she had studied harder.
5 If she were nicer, she'd make more friends.
6 We would have caught the train on time if we had left the house earlier.
7 I'd buy a new car if I had more money.
8 If it hadn't rained yesterday, we would have played tennis.

2

2 I'm doing some research into how children spend their pocket money.
3 In the final set Roger Federer beat Rafael Nadal 6 – 2.
4 I'm terribly sorry, Madam, for making a mistake with your bill.
5 My cousin's really good at languages – she speaks German, French and Russian.
6 Samantha's very worried about her exams.
7 He made a lot of money when he worked in the City of London, but now he's a teacher.
8 We've been working for two hours now, so let's take / have a short break and have a coffee.

3

2 stole   3 miss   4 rises   5 lend   6 currently

Video exercises

Unit 1

a 2 a   3 b

b 2 other family members   3 father

c 2 c   3 b   4 a   5 c   6 b

d 2 speaks several languages   3 colloquial Spanish

Unit 2

a 2 b   3 d   4 a

b 2 b   3 c   4 a

c 2 c   3 b   4 a

d 2 d   3 a   4 b

e 2 Cambridge   3 very different from   4 easy

Unit 3

a 2 c   3 b   4 a

b 2 d   3 b   4 a

c 2 her house   3 he lives a long way away   4 are in the same class

d 2 b   3 c   4 a

e 2 c   3 d   4 b

Unit 4

a 2 d   3 a   4 b

b 2 b   3 b   4 c

c 2 to strangers   3 spelling   4 wears

d 2 b   3 d   4 a

Unit 5

a 2 in the street   3 land   4 the air is   5 cars and lorries   6 isn't very much

b 2 a   3 b   4 a

c 2 b   3 a   4 d

d 2 saving water   3 bad about   4 glass

e 2 b   3 d   4 a

Unit 6

a 2 exciting   3 interesting   4 public transport looks like

b 2 d   3 a   4 c

c 2 d   3 h   4 g   5 a   6 b   7 f   8 e

d 2 a   3 c   4 c

e 2 d   3 a   4 b

Unit 7

a 2 lives   3 people   4 parks for children

b 2 c   3 a   4 b

c 2 a   3 d   4 b

d 2 b   3 b   4 a

Unit 8

a 2 b   3 a   4 c   5 b

b 2 on the train   3 shopping   4 the *Independent*   5 occasionally

c 2 b   3 a   4 e   5 d

d 2 entertainment   3 international   4 local   5 people

e 2 c   3 a   4 a   5 b

Unit 9

a 2 c   3 a   4 b   5 b

b 2 b   3 d   4 a

c 2 several years ago   3 the whole family   4 happy

d 2 d   3 c   4 a

Unit 10

a 2 c   3 a   4 c   5 c

b 2 d   3 a   4 e   5 b

c 2 daughter   3 respects   4 is not interested in   5 for the bus

d 2 d   3 b   4 a   5 c

Acknowledgements

The authors and publishers acknowledge the following sources of copyright material and are grateful for the permissions granted. While every effort has been made, it has not always been possible to identify the sources of all the material used, or to trace all copyright holders. If any omissions are brought to our notice, we will be happy to include the appropriate acknowledgements on reprinting and in the next update to the digital edition, as applicable.

The publisher has used its best endeavours to ensure that the URLs for external websites referred to in this book are correct and active at the time of going to press. However, the publisher has no responsibility for the websites and can make no guarantee that a site will remain live or that the content is or will remain appropriate.

The publishers are grateful to the following for permission to reproduce copyright photographs and material:

Key: L = left, C = centre, R = right, T = top, B = bottom

p.4(TR): Shutterstock/ARENA Creative; p.4(BL): Alamy/allesalltag; p.5(TL): Shutterstock/stefanolunardi; p.5(BR): Shutterstock/Christian Knospe; p.6(T): Shutterstock/TATSIANAMA; p.6(BR): Shutterstock/Ruslan Guzov; p.7(BR): Shutterstock/Iakov Filimonov; p.8(CR): Shutterstock/oneinchpunch; p.9(TL): Shutterstock/f9photos; p.10(BL): Shutterstock/wavebreakmedia; p.11(CL): Shutterstock/Galina Barskaya; p.11(TR): Shutterstock/Patryk Kosmider; p.12(B): Shutterstock/OrelPhoto; p.13(TR): Shutterstock/Stephen Coburn; p.14(TR): Shutterstock/wavebreakmedia; p.15(TL): Shutterstock/racorn; p.16(TL): Shutterstock/2xSamara.com; p.16(BR): Shutterstock/BlueOrange Studio; p.17(TL): Alamy/MBI/Stockbroker; p.17(BL): Alamy/OJO Images Ltd/Robert Nicholas; p.17(BR): Alamy/Janine Wiedel Photolibrary/janine wiedel; p.18(B): Shutterstock/Alan49; p.19(BL): Alamy/ClassicStock/H. ARMSTRONG ROBERTS; p.20(B): Shutterstock/Alex Staroseltsev; p.21(TL): Shutterstock/Johnny Habell; p.22(CL): Shutterstock/Pavel L Photo and Video; p.22(T): Alamy/PCN Photography/PCN Black; p.23(CR): Shutterstock/Visionsi; p.23(TL): Alamy/Kumar Sriskandan; p.23(TR): Shutterstock/RubinowaDama; p.24(BR): Alamy/Johner Images; p.24(TR): Shutterstock/Anton Kudelin; p.25(TR): Alamy/Pontino; p.26(BL): Shutterstock/Maglara; p.28(BL): Alamy/Blend Images/Ronnie Kaufman/Larry Hirshowitz; p.28(TR): Alamy/Lou Linwei; p.29(CL): Shutterstock/Stuart Monk; p.29(1): Shutterstock/Matt Gibson; p.29(2): Shutterstock/LoloStock;

p.29(3): Shutterstock/LauraDyer; p.29(4): Shutterstock/Panu Ruangjan; p.29(5): Shutterstock/italay; p.29(6): Shutterstock/Olha Insight; p.29(7): Shutterstock/wandee007; p.29(8): Shutterstock/Aleksey Stemmer; p.29(9): Shutterstock/Tiago M Nunes; p.30(BL): Shutterstock/MNBB Studio; p.31(TL): Alamy/Travel Pictures/Pictures Colour Library; p.31(B): Shutterstock/Olivier Le Queinec; p.32(B): Shutterstock/Bruce Rolff; p.33(CL): Shutterstock/Concept Photo; p.34(TR): Getty Images/Doug Menuez; p.34(BL): Shutterstock/SK Kim; p.35(CL): Shutterstock/ariadna de raadt; p.35(BR): Shutterstock/Yellowj; p.36(B): Shutterstock/Viacheslav Lopatin; p.36(TR): Shutterstock/antb; p.37(T): Shutterstock/posztos; p.38(CR): Shutterstock/RioPatuca; p.40(CL): Shutterstock/Tyler Olson; p.41(TL): Shutterstock/Adam Gregor; p.41(TR): Alamy/Blend Images/Jade; p.42(TR): Alamy/Inmagine; p.42(BR): Shutterstock/Diego Cervo; p.43(C): Getty Images/Karl Blackwel; p.43(BR): Getty Images/Ekaterina Monakhova; p.44(C): Shutterstock/Darren Brode; p.46(T): Shutterstock/Kiko Calderon ESP; p.47(CL): Shutterstock/Takacs Szabolcs; p.47(TR): Getty Images/Jupiterimages; p.48(BL): Getty Images/Yellow Dog Productions; p.48(TR): Alamy/Geof Kirby; p.49(TR): Alamy/imageBROKER/Martin Schrampf; p.50(CR): Shutterstock/Lopolo; p.50(BR): Shutterstock/Blend Images; p.50(TR): Shuttertsock/wellphoto; p.51(B): Shutterstock/ronstik; p.52(TL): Kobal/Lucasfilm/20th Century Fox; p.52(TR): Getty Images/ABC/Lorenzo Bevilaqua; p.53(TR): Shutterstock/Igor Bulgarin; p.54(TR): Shutterstock/cdrin; p.54(B): Ronald Grant Archive/Walt Disney Pictures/Pixar Animation Studios; p.55(TL): Shutterstock/Air Images; p.55(BR): Shutterstock/Goodluz; p.56(B): Shutterstock/gualtiero boffi; p.57(TL): Shutterstock/stocksolutions; p.58(TL): Shutterstock/MIMOHE; p.58(TR): Shutterstock/arek_malang; p.58(CR): Getty Images/AFP/PAUL ELLIS; p.59(TL): Shutterstock/CHEN WS; p.59(BL): Alamy/P.D. Amedzro; p.59(TR): Shutterstock/Viacheslav Lopatin; p.60(BL): Alamy/Wild Places Photography/Chris Howes; p.60(TR): Alamy/AF archive/A.F. ARCHIVE; p.61(CR): Shutterstock/marchello74; p.62(B): Shutterstock/Rob Hainer.

Video stills by Rob Maidment and Sharp Focus Productions: p.30, 64, 66, 67, 68, 69, 71.

Filming in King's College by kind permission of the Provost and Scholars of King's College, Cambridge.

Illustrations by Ben Swift p. 49; Vicky Woodgate p.12, 19.